THE YORKSHIRE

DALES

NATIONAL PARK

A CELEBRATION OF 60 YEARS

BY COLIN SPEAKMAN

YORKSHIRE DALES
National Park

GREAT NORTHERN

Great Northern Books
PO Box 213, Ilkley, LS29 9WS
www.greatnorthernbooks.co.uk

This book is dedicated to all those men and women who, between 1954 and the present time, have served the Yorkshire Dales National Park Committee and Authority, its communities and its visitors, so very well, whether as Authority Members, Officers or Volunteers.

ISBN: 978-0-9928193-0-9

Design and layout: David Burrill

Title page photo: Upper Swaledale between Keld and Muker. (Mike Kipling)

CIP Data
A catalogue for this book is available
from the British Library

Abbreviations in photo credits:

YDGLA	Yorkshire Dales Green Lanes Alliance
YDMT	Yorkshire Dales Millennium Trust
YDNPA	Yorkshire Dales National Park Authority
YPN	Yorkshire Post Newspapers

Contents

	Preface	5
Chapter One	How It All Began	7
Chapter Two	The Early Years	27
Chapter Three	The National Park comes of Age	41
Chapter Four	Conserving the Barns and Hay Meadows	57
Chapter Five	Saving the Green Lane Lanes	69
Chapter Six	The Green Travel Revolution	77
Chapter Seven	Green Energy - threat or promise?	91
Chapter Eight	Farming in a National Park (Anthony Bradley)	101
Chapter Nine	Unfinished Business	109
Chapter Ten	The Future of the Yorkshire Dales	117
	Acknowledgements	138
	Further Information	138
	Select Bibliography	139
	Index	140
	Subscribers	142

Preface

It has been my good fortune to edit many of the books that Colin Speakman has written over the past forty years. They have embraced his skills as a countryside campaigner and his unique approach to such subjects as walking, transport and 'green' issues. Abundantly clear in so many of them has been his deep love for the Yorkshire Dales National Park.

Such enthusiasm is not surprising. The special qualities of the area were admirably summarised in an earlier Great Northern book on the Dales, which Colin and I jointly compiled to mark the new Millennium. In his foreword, the Prince of Wales commented: 'With its potent mix of rolling fells, deep valleys, swirling rivers and limestone scars, all bound together by a rich tapestry of drystone walls, the Dales is rightly regarded as one of the most treasured landscapes in Britain.'

It is these qualities that led to the core of the Dales becoming a National Park in 1954. This book commemorates the 60th anniversary of its designation in three distinct ways. Firstly, it provides a much needed history of the Park, which has inevitably had its 'downs' as well as its 'ups'. Yet Colin is able to conclude: 'The story of the Yorkshire Dales National Park over the last sixty years has been a remarkable one, something to be both proud of and to celebrate.'

A second part of the text looks at some key issues that have had to be addressed and largely resolved in positive ways. They include the saving of barns, drystone walls and hay meadows threatened with oblivion; preventing the destruction of many 'green lanes' by off-road vehicles; responding to a new era of travel; and meeting ever-pressing demands for renewable energy. A chapter by 'guest author' and working farmer Anthony Bradley looks at the challenges of farming in a National Park.

Finally, these pages also form a visual celebration. At the outset Colin and I agreed that he would write the text and I would choose the illustrations. This would not be yet another tourist guide to the Yorkshire Dales full of pretty pictures. Instead, the photographs have been chosen specifically to relate to points made in the text, with the addition of archive images that capture the area and its people some sixty years ago.

I hope that the words and illustrations will collectively be seen as a worthy celebration of the Yorkshire Dales National Park on its 60th anniversary.

David Joy
Editor

Swinnergill Falls, one of the many superb waterfalls that are such a feature of the Yorkshire Dales National Park. (Welcome to Yorkshire)

Sheep are driven through Malham for the annual
sheep sale. A distinctive car is hauling the farm
trailer but not another vehicle is in sight in this
scene from the 1950s. (David Joy collection)

Chapter One

How It All Began

1954. A cool wet, summer. Britain slowly emerging from the after effects of a long and punishing World War – food rationing had just finally ended, the wartime leader Winston Churchill was Prime Minister, Roger Bannister ran a mile in under four minutes, Bill Haley and the Comets were about to start the Rock 'n Roll craze, the world's first atomic power station opened in Russia, but slightly more ominously a little known military leader Colonel Nasser seized power in Egypt – and would soon take action leading to the closure of the Suez Canal and a disastrous war that would mark the decline of Britain's importance as an Imperial power.

Britain sixty years ago was a very different country from that of today. Living standards from the perspective of people of Britain in the early twenty-first century would seem abysmally low. Most people lived in houses without central heating, many had no bathrooms and outside loos. Horses and carts were still a common sight on city streets, as were elderly trams though these were being rapidly replaced by motor buses. Cars were still a luxury to be enjoyed by the more affluent. But their numbers were growing rapidly. There were around 6 million vehicles on Britain's roads (compared with 34 million in 2011).

Town and cities, especially in the industrial North of England, were almost universally black in appearance, resulting from decades of dense smoke from domestic coal-burning grates, factory chimneys and elderly steam locomotives coating buildings and any washing hanging out to dry. Dense lung-choking eye-watering fog was a common experience throughout the winter months. The Clean Air Act was still two years away.

Yet despite all privations and discomforts of life in Britain in the early 1950s, there was a buzz of optimism in the air. Year by year things were getting better. People suddenly had more money in their pockets, more things to buy. Acquiring the seeming scientific miracle of television, hugely boosted since the first televised Coronation of Queen Elizabeth two years previously, was an aspiration for most families. Consumer goods such as washing machines and fridges were for the first time affordable for most working families – albeit mostly only acquired by regular higher purchase payments.

National Parks were part of the UK post war settlement, with the great burst of radical legislation and social change of the 1940s that brought about such wonders as the National Health Service, free secondary education for all, and the great 1947 Town and Country Planning Act which safeguarded the countryside from urban sprawl. Yet during the 1950s and '60s, there was to be a boom in new house building with the demolition of crowded city centre slums to be replaced by new overspill housing estates on the edge of cities, and creation of new 'garden cities' in the open countryside.

More controversially perhaps, basic industries such as coal mining, energy, steel, road and rail transport were nationalised. Most historians would argue that given the huge scale reconstruction and renewal that was necessary, state intervention on the scale that was needed was the only option at that time, even if it eventually became clear that the creation of large, inefficient state monopolies were not to provide the solution to Britain's economic woes.

The fact that the post war Attlee Government, faced with so many intractable problems, including shortages of basic resources, was able to deliver some of the most far reaching legislation in our history, in terms of both protecting the countryside and making it accessible to the nation's urban millions, was truly astonishing.

It could only happen because of a remarkable idealism. It came about because of the influence of a small group of single minded individuals who during the 1920s and '30s, and right through the darkest years of the Second World War, when the very survival of Britain as a nation was threatened, worked both within and outside Government to change opinion and finally even help devise the legislation needed to create National Parks.

National Parks were not a British invention, though the concept owes its origin to the ideas of a great English poet, walker and thinker, William Wordsworth, who in the 1835 edition of his influential *Guide to the Lakes* suggested that the Lake District should be regarded as a '*sort of national property in which every man has a right and interest who has an eye to perceive and a heart to enjoy*'. But it was in the United States, not the United Kingdom, that the first 'National Park' was created at Yellowstone in 1870.

America, and indeed many other countries of the world soon to follow that example, was a very different country from small, long developed and crowded Britain. There were huge areas of virgin countryside, true wilderness still to be settled and tamed, but already by the mid-19th century at risk from industrial exploitation and agricultural expansion. It took the writer, campaigner and early environmentalist John Muir to teach people the true value of wilderness, both as a way of protecting nature and wildlife, and as a spiritual sanctuary for modern man, leading to the creation in 1890 of Yosemite, one of the world's most spectacular National Parks.

Wilderness National Parks, in which protection of wildlife and biodiversity were paramount, was the model which spread throughout the world, including in many other European countries. In England and Wales true wilderness no longer exists – even the wildest summits of Snowdonia, Dartmoor, the Lake District, Peak District or the Yorkshire Dales were

John Dower, who brilliantly articulated the case for National Parks.

tamed by woodland clearance, sheep walks, reservoirs, forests, towns, roads, and even quarries. Scotland which still contains many true wilderness areas, was eventually to have a different National Park tradition of its own.

Nevertheless, the idea of an appropriate form of National Park for England and Wales, based as much on a cultural heritage of well-loved landscapes as on wildlife conservation, soon began to gain support among the many voluntary organisations that formed the UK outdoor movement. These included the National Trust and many organisations which were developed in this important between-wars period - the Council to Protect Rural England, the Ramblers Association, the Youth Hostels Association, the Holiday Fellowship and Countrywide Holidays

Association (CHA) and the Friends of the Lake District.

These were some of the bodies that established the Standing Committee on National Parks (now the Campaign for National Parks) which was created in 1936 to bring together many of the leading voluntary organisations to represent the interests of walkers, cyclists, youth hostellers and country lovers to secure legislation that would establish National Parks in England and Wales – Scotland was to await another two generations.

Two remarkable individuals probably did more than any others to lead the campaign to make National Parks in England and Wales a reality.

The first was John Dower, an architect and planner from Ilkley, West Yorkshire who as the first Drafting Secretary of the Standing Committee, not only was able to brilliantly articulate the case for National Parks and countryside protection in England and Wales, but was able to brief key influential Government committees. Invalided out of the War with the tuberculosis which was to cause his premature death in 1947, Dower spent the war years in a cottage in Kirkby Malham, researching and writing what was to become the great Dower Report which was to set the scene for National Parks in England and Wales.

The Yorkshire Dales played a small, but perhaps crucial role in the development of the British concept of National Parks as lived-in cultural landscapes not just nature protection areas without a local population. Whilst he was working on his report, Dower spoke with local farmers, and was well aware of the great contribution hill farming and local culture made to the special landscape qualities of the area, and how supporting hill farming communities was essential to the National Park. He was also frequently joined by his fellow Quaker, the celebrated landscape historian and industrial archaeologist Arthur Raistrick. Raistrick would regularly walk over to Kirkby Malham from his home in Linton to spend hours with Dower, the two of them discussing what was required to be in the hoped-for legislation not just for National Parks but for nature protection, public rights of way, long

distance paths and public access to the countryside.

John Dower's report, published in 1945, and generally referred to as the Dower Report, remains a seminal document for anyone who cares for National Parks and the British countryside.

The other hero of the National Park movement came from Burnley, Lancashire on the other side of the Pennines, the journalist and campaigner Tom Stephenson. Tom, yet another Quaker and conscientious objector who suffered for his beliefs, became an outdoor correspondent on a popular national daily newspaper *The Daily Herald*, which Tom used to promote his ideas about National Parks, access to the countryside, and long distance footpaths such as the Pennine Way.

During the war Tom became the Press Secretary for the new Ministry of Town and Country Planning, as well as remaining active in the Ramblers Association. This enabled him to work closely with politicians, some of whom became senior figures in the post-war Labour Government. These included Lewis Silkin, the new Minister for Town and Country Planning. Silkin asked Stephenson to join Sir Arthur Hobhouse's Committee on National Parks which reported in 1947 and which endorsed all of John Dower's key recommendations, including the radical measures to survey and record all public rights of way in England and Wales.

Most of these recommendations – including proposals for a Yorkshire Dales National Park – were eventually to find their way into the great National Parks and Access to the Countryside Act of 1949. But this Act might not have got onto the statute book had it not been for Stephenson's brilliant campaigning work in 1948, speaking, writing, organising mass letter writing. Perhaps most crucial of all, Tom arranged a three day walking trip in the Peak District along a section of the proposed Pennine Way with Hugh Dalton, then Chancellor of the Exchequer and a highly influential member of the Cabinet, and rising young backbench stars Fred Willey, Barbara Castle, and Arthur Blenkinsop. During this trip Dalton was persuaded, despite a crowded agenda, to prioritise the National Park Bill in the last months of the Attlee Government before the 1950 General Election.

The two core purposes of National Parks as set out in the Bill were 'to conserve and enhance the natural beauty, wildlife and cultural heritage' of the designated areas and 'to promote opportunities for the understanding and enjoyment of the special qualities of the park'. These two great purposes still provide the cornerstone of all work in every National Park in England and Wales.

As well as providing the legislative powers to create National Parks, the Bill set up the National Parks Commission (later to became the Countryside Commission/Agency and now Natural England), Areas of Outstanding Natural Beauty, National Nature Reserves, Long Distance Footpaths and measures to create what are now the great Definitive Maps of Rights of Way in every county of England and Wales.

The Act became law in December 1949 just a few weeks before the 1950 election in which the Labour Government was re-elected with only a tiny majority. But this was sufficient to allow this administration to create the first UK National Parks. The very first to be established was the Peak District in April 1951, to be followed a few weeks afterwards by the Lake District.

However riven by internal dissent, and in an attempt to shore up his authority and secure a larger majority, Attlee went to the country in October of that year. But dealing with a fatally divided opposition, the Conservatives could not believe their luck and went on to win the election with a small but adequate majority of 17. One of the last acts of the Labour Government was the creation of Snowdonia and Dartmoor National Parks just days before the election on October 26.

Though it was feared that the new administration with their traditional support among landowners and with a senior Cabinet member such as Harold Macmillan, the new Minister for Housing and Local Government, a keen grouse moor sportsman, might be hostile to the concept of public access to moorland and National Parks, it was soon clear that National Parks now enjoyed strong cross-party support. The new Government would continue to deliver them to the nation.

In 1952 there followed the North York Moors and the Pembrokeshire Coast National Parks, but the Yorkshire Dales had to wait the third tranche, in November 1954, a month after Exmoor's designation. It was therefore the eighth to be created and not without some difficulty.

The new National Park in the Yorkshire Dales was proposed to cover some 683 square miles (1,769 square kilometres) within the territory of what were at that time (prior to the 1974 changes) two ancient Yorkshire counties, the old North Riding and the old West Riding.

The idea of a National Park in the Yorkshire Dales went back some 23 years previously when in 1931 suggestions were made by planners Patrick Abercrombie and Dr Vaughan Cornish and the Manchester & District Joint Town Planning Committee to the Addison Committee on National Parks about a Yorkshire Dales National Park. The suggestions were made that areas of the Yorkshire Pennines mainly in Craven, including Malham, Kilnsey and Ingleton but also part of Swaledale, should be made into a National Park. Nothing happened over the next decade, but the idea was eventually taken up by John Dower in his 1945 Report. Dower proposed three protected landscapes within what is now the Yorkshire Dales National Park – an area including the Upper Wharfe, Aire and Ribble valleys of some 380 square miles which he thought should be 'Division A' or highest priority for designation, and in 'Division B' two areas – what he described as the Swaledale Pennines (which also included parts of Wensleydale) to cover some 240 square miles, and 280 square miles of the Howgill Fells and the Upper Lune Valley (though not Dentdale).

The Hobhouse Report of 1947 combined these three proposals into one major protected landscape, much closer to the boundaries of the National Park that were eventually designated, though surprisingly still excluding Dentdale and the Howgills which were envisaged as a separate 'conservation area'.

But the proposals for a National Park in the Yorkshire Dales finally began to firm up in July 1952, when a special visit was arranged to the Yorkshire

Dales by members of the new National Parks Commission. The deputation included Tom Stephenson and Mrs Pauline Dower, widow of John and a passionate conservationist in her own right.

This group rightly decided that both Dentdale and at least the southern boundary of the Howgills that was in the old West Riding should come into the National Park, and whilst some areas west of Richmond and Leyburn were excluded, they were able to ensure that beautiful Coverdale came into the new Park. The criteria they adopted were on grounds of 'landscape quality', an inevitably subjective value-judgement, but a core principle which is just as relevant when discussing future National Park designations or boundary variations today.

After due formalities and procedures, the Commission were able to put forward concrete proposals for the Yorkshire Dales National Park to Government for formal consultation in the form of a Designation Order. This then had to be taken forward to a Public Inquiry before a Planning Inspector who would finally make his recommendations known to Government. After the usual processes this Inquiry finally took place in May 1954.

There were quite a lot of objections. Interestingly the proposed designation was virulently opposed by both County Councils – a classic case of local politicians and bureaucrats defending their territory, resisting any attempt to take away their power, control and influence; reactions now echoed at the present time over the issue of extending the existing Yorkshire Dales National Park boundaries northwards and westwards. At the Public Inquiry held in May 1954 to discuss the proposals, the then Chief Planning Officer of West Riding County Council claimed that the contribution of £2,800 already being made by his authority to the sections of the Peak District National Park within the West Riding was 'a complete waste of money'.

Many rural communities in the Dales and elsewhere saw the imposition of a National Park simply as the heavy hand of national Government interfering with local democracy. There was a view,

Arthur Raistrick photographed in 1975. (YDNPA)

still held in many communities, that National Parks were all about the urban majority invading and imposing their will on rural communities. As one town clerk in the North Riding expressed it: "National Parks are not generally desired. It is a scheme of fanatics, idealists and those out of touch with life in the countryside."

Opposition was especially strong too from the old Corporation Water Boards who alleged that allowing public access to the main moorland catchment areas was a major risk to public health – for example of typhoid – from sewage leaks or pollution. This was one reason for the exclusion of the magnificent moors of Upper Nidderdale, of outstanding landscape quality yet which did not feature in either Hobhouse or Dower, from the Yorkshire Dales National Park. The area, much of it owned by Bradford Corporation, had to wait for protection until 1990 with the designation of the Nidderdale Area of Outstanding Natural Beauty. Better filtration systems have long removed any supposed pollution risks caused by public access to water catchment areas.

Opposition to designation also came from the local National Farmers' Union who saw this as a threat to their members' livelihoods. It was claimed that National Parks would lead to 'hoards' of trespassing visitors from the cities walking across their members' fields and moorland pastures, disturbing livestock, spreading TB among attested herds of cattle, damaging walls, leaving gates open and dropping heaps of litter everywhere. At the Public Inquiry the solicitor engaged by the NFU arrived with a sackful of litter which he claimed had been left by visitors at or near the lakeside at Semerwater, Wensleydale, which he then proceeded to shake out on the table in front of the Inspector in a dramatic gesture of protest.

Other reasons include the statement by both local authorities that a National Park was not needed as they were doing all the necessary planning work and no extra expenditure would be required.

However, the Inspector, Mr W.N. Cortis, was not impressed with such arguments nor those of the water authorities. In his report, he indicated that he fully supported the proposals of the National Parks Commission for a Yorkshire Dales National Park and considered that the areas under consideration fully 'complied with the requirements of the 1949 Act' and that the Designation Order should be confirmed.

This was duly acted upon by Government and on October 12th, 1954 the Order creating the National Park was finally confirmed to come into being on November 16th, subject to any final appeal within six weeks to the High Court. None was received and the Yorkshire Dales finally became a National Park.

But once the celebrations had died down and campaigners began to read the small print, it was clear that what had been gained was compromised in two vital ways – inadequate finance and weak governance.

Part of the problem lay in the fact that a significant percentage of the costs of the new National Park were to come by precept from the local authorities. This was in direct contradiction to the recommendations of the Hobhouse Committee which had indicated that National Parks being for the nation should be financed by the nation, not the unfortunate ratepayers of the area where the Park happened to be situated. Originally this was planned to come from a £50 million endowment – a huge sum of money in the currency values of the time – in a National Land Fund especially set up by Hugh Dalton in 1949 when he was Chancellor, as a 'nest egg' to cover the full costs of establishing and operating National Parks. However, in 1955 the then Conservative administration returned this bounty – now with added interest – back to the Exchequer to be used for other purposes.

A further weakening of the intentions of the founding fathers came in the loophole in the 1949 Act. The initial intention was to administer the new National Park with strong, independent Joint Boards which consisted of both locally elected members nominated by the relevant local authorities, and a smaller number of individuals nominated by the relevant Government Minister because of their specialist expertise and local knowledge, for example local historians, ecologists or people with close links to the amenity movement. This is what happened in the first two National Parks, the Peak District and Lake District, both established in 1951. However the legislation also allowed 'by reason of special circumstances', for a much weaker Committee structure to be set up, in effect embedded within and ultimately controlled by the local authority.

Not surprisingly, local authorities were quick to argue that 'special circumstances' applied to their area. Government in turn recognised that by not insisting, as they had in the Peak and the Lakes, in the setting up of Joint Boards to administer the new Parks, then some of the resistance by local authorities to having a National Park, as they saw it imposed on them, would melt away. This meant that the governance of all the National Parks designated after 1952, including the Yorkshire Dales, was in the hands of bodies that were, in effect, subcommittees of the relevant local authority, though with some national funding and with the Ministerially appointed members to represent the wider national interest.

National Park campaigners felt betrayed. The much hoped for new National Parks, with the

Country lovers welcomed the designation of the Yorkshire Dales National Park in 1954. It says much for its success that the landscape quality remains largely unchanged. This view looks from Askrigg across Wensleydale to the distinctive flat-topped peak of Addlebrough. (Welcome to Yorkshire)

possible exception of the Peak and Lake District with their own independent Boards, would be underfunded and administered, as in the case of both the Yorkshire Dales and North York Moors National Parks, by the very same bodies that had initially opposed their very existence.

In the Yorkshire Dales this was to lead to the absurd situation of there being two National Park Committees – one for the West Riding section and one for the North Riding, both with their own separate ideas, policies and practices and officers, though these were eventually – in 1957 – to be coordinated with a token Joint Advisory Committee consisting of representatives of both bodies.

Nevertheless, when the news of the designation of the Yorkshire Dales National Park was announced, there was quiet rejoicing among environmentalists.

It might be a much weaker and less effective body than had been hoped for, but at least there was now a National Park for the Yorkshire Dales. As Arthur Raistrick, who was to serve for many years on the West Riding Committee of the National Park, wrote on hearing the news: "At last the Yorkshire Dales National Park is designated and confirmed to the delight of all country lovers....We welcome the Park; it offers all that we want, country for the walker, ranging from the wildest fell tops to the pleasant riverside walks of the lower dales.... It is a paradise for the naturalist and geologist, and we who live in it and know it, believe that any right-minded person, whatever his country taste, can find satisfaction within its bounds."

Focus on the 1950s

Thanks in considerable measure to the Yorkshire Dales National Park, much of the landscape has changed little in the last sixty years. Inevitably the way of life is very different as depicted in these photographs from the 1950s (and a few from the '60s).

Sheep shearing at Raisgill Farm, Langstrothdale, in July 1966 was an occasion for a gathering of willing hands. (Marie Hartley & Joan Ingilby)

Hand shearing at West Scale Park, Kettlewell, with H Plews making the last cut. (Bertram Unné)

Hand milking of cattle was also very common in the 1950s. Bryan White seems happy in his task at Linton, Wharfedale. (John S Murray)

Two members of the Harper family handling hay at Dandra Garth, Garsdale. Once loaded the sledge would be taken by a horse to the nearest barn. (Marie Hartley & Joan Ingilby)

Haytime at Bainbridge in the days when the grass was still made into foot-cocks. This laborious process involved drawing the hay over a raised foot with a rake before putting a second layer on top that acted as a thatch in poor weather. (John Edenbrow)

Farm life in the Dales in the 1950s. Herbert Bentham and his family turning hay by hand at Dockle Sike Farm, Deepdale, near Dent. It only needed to rain and they would have to start all over again. (Geoffrey N. Wright)

One of the finest photographs ever taken of 'drinkings', when those toiling in the hayfield took a break for refreshment. From left to right in this Deepdale scene are Herbert Bentham, Allan & Betty Middleton, their children Joyce, Shirley and Joan, and Allan Middleton senior. (Geoffrey N Wright)

A horse and cart deliver a load of manure to what appears to be a newly established garden at Keld. (Bertram Unné)

A long-handled scythe is used by Mr Hunter of Keld to cut his meadowland. (Tom Parker)

Apart from hay, horses also handled bracken which was used in barns as bedding in the winter months. Seen here is a very full load in Garsdale. (Bertam Unné)

This could be most of the population of the tiny village of Horsehouse in Coverdale, lined up outside the shop and post office to chat with the vicar. (R B Fawcett)

Cattle are driven along the main street on Hawes market day, when such a sight was once commonplace. (Bertram Unné)

Traditional shop scene at Thoralby in Bishopdale. Much of the wall space is taken up by a Post Office poster with the message 'This Land of ours – Save for it!' (Bertram Unné)

Lingering on into the 1950s were passenger services on the Wensleydale branch line. Sadly there is little sign of life in this view of a two-coach train at Hawes. (J W Armstrong Trust)

Country dress and footwear was not ideal when this group was photographed at Gordale Scar. The path to the Scar was then not up to today's standards. (G H Hesketh)

The library service is today fighting for survival. It was a busy scene when the West Riding County Council mobile library made its weekly visit to Appletreewick in Wharfedale. (Clifford Robinson)

Three walkers stride away from Horton in Ribblesdale with Penyghent in the background. This photograph was included in Colin Speakman's earlier book Walk! – A Celebration of Striding Out and brought an email from Margaret Chadwick regarding the time she was walking with two friends in the 1950s: "We were meeting the rest of the mountaineering club from Blackpool for a scramble on Arncliffe rocks. I have been walking in the countryside and mountaineering since I was 15. I am now 81 and was honoured to appear in the same book as my heroes Ben Fogle and Chris Bonington.
(David Joy collection)

HIGH CLASS GROCERIES
HARDWARE & HOUSEHOLD GOODS
BUCKDEN POST OFFICE

James Farshaw

STATIONARY AND LOCAL VIEWS

NEWSAGENT LICENCED to SELL
TOBACCO PATENT MEDICINES
PETROL AND MOTOR OILS

Sign of the times at Buckden, with the shop and post office still licensed to sell tobacco and patent medicines as well as petrol and motor oils. (David Joy collection)

Chapter Two

The Early Years

Our National Parks – the highest category of landscape protection – are the most iconic areas of Britain's countryside. Our deep love and affection for them helps to define us as English, Welsh or Scottish people. Talk to any moderately articulate English person about what England means to them, and within a few minutes there will be reference to the Lake District, South Downs, Peak District, Northumberland, Dartmoor, Exmoor, New Forest, North York Moors or the Yorkshire Dales. Expect any Welsh person to feel the same way about Snowdonia, Pembrokeshire or the Brecon Beacons, or Scot about the Cairngorms or Loch Lomond. These are the areas of our island that most help to shape our sense of belonging to our nation.

Incalculable too is the economic value of our National Parks – the billions which pour into the national economy as visitors from other parts of the UK and from overseas, come to stay, walk, cycle, or simply absorb the beauty of landscapes which have inspired some of our greatest literature and most evocative paintings.

The mystery is why it took so long for the nation to fully recognise this, not only to pass the necessary laws to protect and enhance these magnificent areas for present and future generations, but to ensure that adequate resources, human and financial, were there to deliver what was so close to our deepest beliefs about our culture and identity.

Yet National Parks – our highest category of landscape protection – have always been underfunded compared with say, the visual arts or buildings. A national appeal to ensure that a painting by a great Italian artist stays in Britain often attracts more money from public and private funders than the protection of the magnificent landscapes that have inspired so many of our own greatest artists.

When the Yorkshire Dales National Park finally came into being at the end of 1954 that was only the start of the process of creating a true National Park. It was not fully anticipated at the time that for some years to come the Park would remain little more than a line on a map. Nor could it be assumed that an invisible line on the ground offered any kind of protection. Was it ever sensible to assume that a piece of countryside on one side of a line was nationally important whilst that on the other side of the line was not?

As several commentators have pointed out, the problem was that in Britain, few people understood what the words 'National Park' actually meant. They were not 'national' in the sense that most other National Parks overseas are, owned by the state or one of its agencies. The land was not in any kind of national or quasi-national ownership. Around 98% was and remains in private hands. Nor were they 'parks' in the normally understood meaning of the word as an open area of public land where you could wander around freely, as in an urban park. Even in fairly recent times, it was not uncommon for someone to come into a National Park Information Centre in the Dales and ask 'where is the park?' looking for a boating lake and swings.

If visitors got it wrong, misconceptions were equally entrenched within the local community. The Town and Country Planning Act was introduced in 1947, just before the National Parks Act. People living in the Dales frequently (and often still) imagined that planning regulations were uniquely applied in National Parks, not elsewhere, somehow unfairly imposed on them by Government to prevent them building or erecting whatever they liked

Ingleborough National Nature Reserve is one of several rigorously protected wildlife habitats and botanic reserves within the National Park. Tom Ducket is fixing a key notice on one of the Reserve's gateways at Scar Close Moss. (Natural England)

wherever they liked on their own land. The more prosaic truth is that planning regulations within and outside National Parks are identical, but are applied more rigorously and are subject to tighter policies than outside the Park boundaries.

But because National Parks were created relatively late in Britain, the international name was constantly used by campaigners and legislators until it became common currency. To try and call our Parks 'Areas of National Protection' or 'Landscape Heritage Areas' just wouldn't work. The name had already stuck.

If the name confused many visitors in the Yorkshire Dales National Park, it irritated and annoyed many local people. This is a farmed, forested, quarried landscape, containing not just villages but small towns such as Sedbergh and Hawes, communities where people go about their daily lives. The notion that the National Park should be regarded as some kind of museum, its inhabitants to be gawped at like animals in a zoo, was deeply resented.

In practice, as any reading of the legislation makes clear, the UK concept of a National Park was deeply linked to values of education and spiritual enlightenment, where people from the town and cities, especially young people, could benefit and be inspired by great landscapes and open spaces, from the study of nature. Particularly important were the benefits of outdoor education, understanding and using the countryside for health-giving physical activity, whether it was hill walking, climbing, caving, canoeing or cycling. But again this brought resentment that a National Park should be regarded as some kind of playground where urban people, kitted out in expensive outdoor clothing, should come and enjoy themselves on the same hills and rocky slopes where hill farmers have to struggle to make a living on thin soils and in a harsh climate.

What the UK legislators had created, perhaps inadvertently, was a mechanism to protect what is essentially a cultural landscape. In international nature protection terms, this might be merely a 'Category V' classification of protection, but this offered every opportunity to create even more rigorously protected wildlife habitats and botanic reserves within the cultural landscape, as was soon to happen on the slopes of Ingleborough with the small Colt Park Wood Nature Reserve (now part of the Ingleborough National Nature Reserve), at Ling Gill on the headwaters of the Ribble, or at Malham Tarn, which as well as being an NNR is now an internationally recognised wetland site under the Ramsar convention.

But in 1954 few people understood any of this.

The original intention of the 1949 Act was that the new National Parks, where they crossed local authority boundaries, should be administered by strong, independent Joint Planning Boards. If any National Park Authority in the UK required a Joint Planning Board it was the Yorkshire Dales. It straddled two separate counties, the North and the West Ridings, each having an approximately equal area within their boundaries.

Though both were part of the ancient county of Yorkshire, it is difficult to imagine two local authority areas that could be more different. York was once the northern capital of England, the kingdom of Jorvik, the northern part of Viking-dominated Danelaw covering much of the east and northern areas of Anglo-Saxon England. This territory north of the Humber, with its own traditions and guttural dialects, was eventually in more settled times divided for administrative purposes, following Norse custom, into three 'thrydings' or 'thirds'. These eventually became the counties of North, East and West Riding which survived until 1974. The historic city of York remained an independent City or County Borough, without any allegiance to a Riding.

The old West Riding County Council, created in 1889 with its county town of Wakefield, was by far the largest and powerful of the three local authorities. Their area of jurisdiction extended from the Peak District south of Sheffield along the south and central Pennines almost to the Lake District and Lancashire coast. Even though the cities and larger towns, independent County or Municipal Boroughs, were excluded, most of the satellite towns, villages or suburbs came under West Riding administration, representing a population of 1.9 million people, plus an additional 1.8 million people living in the independent Boroughs.

West Riding therefore included much of the great industrial heartlands of the North. A focus for excellence in manufacturing – steel, textiles, engineering as well as mining, it was a powerful and progressive local authority, with a national reputation for excellence in many fields, most notably education. But there was also a huge rural hinterland, extending northwards to cover most of the Craven Dales as far as the Lune Gorge and the Eastern Dales as far as Ripon.

North Riding County Council was essentially a rural administration, its headquarters the small county town of Northallerton. This was a countryside of rich farmland, ancestral estates and sleepy villages, whose inhabitants even if they no longer worked on the land, owed allegiances to a comfortable social order that went back to medieval times, a world captured with great accuracy by novelist Winifred Holtby in her novel *South Riding*, though this was more about the former East Riding than the North. Market towns such as Thirsk, Masham, Malton, Richmond, Helmsley, Pickering, Hawes and Leyburn reflected a comfortable way of life deeply rooted in rural ways. This contrasted however with the bustling coastal resorts of Scarborough and Whitby where seaside landlords and entrepreneurs brought more urban attitudes, reflected by their elected members. Nevertheless, with a population of North Riding recorded in 1971 as a modest 329,000, this was less than a tenth of the combined population of West Riding County and of the great cities and towns that lay within its geographic area.

In effect therefore until local government changes in 1974, there were two National Parks for the Yorkshire Dales; a West Riding and a North Riding National Park.

The 1949 Act required planning authorities within National Parks to consult the National Park Commission within three months of the Designation on administrative arrangements for the new Park. Though there was a meeting in January 1955, the two authorities decided to press ahead with their demand to the Minister that instead of a Joint Board

for the Yorkshire Dales, a Joint Advisory Committee be set up, which of course would have far less powers.

By then, Duncan Sandys had replaced Harold Macmillan as Minister for Housing and Local Government. Sandys accepted the views of the National Park Commission that a Joint Board was needed, but also was persuaded by the argument of greater costs of a Board, the main burden of which was still coming from local ratepayers. So the compromise was that he would agree to 'postpone' the setting up of a Board because of financial constraints at the time, and in the meantime there would be a Joint Advisory Committee for the Dales, but this would be reviewed in three years' time. Needless to say this review never took place.

Finally after much bureaucratic paperwork, the Joint Advisory Committee had its first meeting, in September 1957, almost three years after the Park had been designated, a dreadful example of filibustering by local authorities to delay the wishes of Parliament.

The Committee was to meet at least four times a year and its work was limited to advising the two authorities on such matters as changes to County Council Development Plans, major industrial or mineral developments, and any other matters requested by the two individual County Council National Park Committees that had also been established by this time.

These two National Park Committees were in effect sub-committees of their local authorities and had delegated powers given to them by the respective County Council to deal with Town and Country Planning matters in their respective areas (in effect Development Control) and other powers and duties required by the 1949 Act. The West Riding Committee finally first met in April 1957, the North Riding Committee only in July 1957.

Each Committee consisted of 18 members, 12 nominated by the County Council from among their elected members, but six nominated by the Minister. Among key Ministerial appointments to the West Riding Committee were Arthur Dower, brother of John Dower and an active and persuasive member of the Dower dynasty, and Arthur Raistrick. The two County Council Committees would nominate the members of the JAC, keeping the same ratio of elected members and appointees.

From all accounts, from the very beginning, the West Riding Committee took their business seriously. Site visits were arranged for members to get to know the area, and on one famous occasion, when the Committee went to view their territory, a bluff former miner, now County Councillor from South Yorkshire, was heard to take a sharp intake of breath when he first saw Malham Cove. "Who quarried that?" was his question.

Quarrying was, in fact, one of the first big challenges facing the new Committee. It was soon discovered, that as soon it seemed, after 1950, that a National Park might indeed be created in the Yorkshire Dales, developers had been quick to get their applications in for new or extended planning permissions for limestone quarrying, especially in Upper Ribblesdale and Upper Wharfedale, before the Park could be designated. These for later generations of planners became ticking time bombs, major problems which could only be prevented at huge cost and legal activity to rescind an existing permission.

Reports were that the old North Riding Committee were much more relaxed about their role, and generally happy to let their planning officers get on with it, which in later years led to suggestions that a lot more bungalows were built in the old North Riding section than the West, which being closer to the major centres of population, had always been under much more intensive pressure both from visitor activity and building development demands. One mischievous story suggested that when the Test Match was on, officers in the North Riding were instructed to get through the business briskly to ensure that members could get round to the serious business of watching the cricket on television.

Neither the North nor the West Riding Committees had their own staff. All matters were dealt with by the relevant County Council planning officers, for whom the National Park matters were just an additional duty, not necessarily their highest priority. But it was the vexed issue of public access

to open countryside that was to force a major change in the way people began to perceive the National Park.

For decades, the Ramblers Association in particular had been campaigning for open access to the open moorland and mountains of England and Wales, and the north of England, with magnificent areas of grouse moorland within easy reach of town and cities, where the demand was highest. This was focused on the magnificent heather moors of Barden Moor and Fell, part of the Duke of Devonshire's extensive Chatsworth Trust estates in the Bolton Abbey area in the south of the new National Park.

Even after the 1949 Act, with its important Part V measures dealing with Access to Open Countryside having been passed, action was painfully slow. The West Riding Chief Planning Officer had indicated that in his opinion there was no need for any action. The Chatsworth Estate had a system of permits. You could write to them to obtain a permit and if there was no shooting taking place on that particular day, permission would be granted. It was not a situation that the Ramblers Association were happy with. After various meetings and fruitless protests, in summer 1958 they decided to call what in effect was a national rally on Ilkley Moor, on the edge of the National Park. Ilkley Moor was chosen not only because of its easy accessibility from both the West Riding and Lancashire, but because it was a piece of open urban common land, owned by Ilkley Council to which the public had enjoyed full legal rights of access for many decades. Yet this was still a grouse moor, with sheep grazing and water catchment, living proof that public access was not incompatible with other legitimate activities on open moorland.

The event was a huge success. Over 2,000 people turned up to listen to Tom Stephenson, Arthur Dower, Arthur Blenkinsop and Arthur Raistrick each making passionate pleas for the access measures of the 1949 Act to be implemented. Within weeks, negotiations were open with the Chatsworth Estate and an Access Agreement was finally negotiated. Gradually, from 1960 onwards, in carefully managed stages, different areas of the moorland were opened up to the public on non-shooting days, subject to

Malham Cove, once embarrassingly mistaken for a quarry by visiting members of a National Park committee! (Simon Hulme – YPN]

rigorous bylaws which allowed the moor to be closed at times of high fire risk, dogs to be forbidden and damaging and anti-social behaviour to be controlled. The final sections of the Barden Moor and Fell Access Agreement only came into being in 1974 but this was to prove a model of its kind. It included bylaws to prevent such matters as fire risk, litter and dogs out of control. In fact over the years there has been little or no damage which could be directly attributed to visitors, most of whom keep to well marked paths rather than walking over the heather.

Now to implement the new Access Agreement Bylaws required someone to be there to enforce these by-laws – a Warden. And so, in 1963, the West Riding Committee took the decision to appoint its first member of staff, Wilf Proctor. Wilf, a telecommunications engineer from Nottingham, soon became a familiar figure with his Land Rover not just in the Barden area but throughout the West Riding area of the Park. He soon realised that the job involved far more than patrolling the moors looking for miscreants or collecting litter, but a wider role of being the representative of the National Park, its face to the outside world both to the visiting public, but equally important to local farmers and landowners.

As Wilf was later to relate, he very much had to create his own job – he was given a Land Rover and a badge and basically had to work out what the job

Wilf Proctor, appointed as the first Warden of the Dales National Park in 1963, repairs a signpost on the Barden Moor and Fell Access Area. (David Joy)

Wilf Proctor was given a Land Rover – and then left to work out what his job entailed. (David Joy)

entailed. Among walkers the idea of a Warden was not universally welcomed. As one rambler remarked: "we spent years fighting gamekeepers trying to keep us off the fells and now we have to deal with Wardens."

But Wilf was soon to recognise that there was a lot more to the job than being some kind of moorland policeman. By 1965 he began to recruit the first of his team of Voluntary Wardens to help carry out the legally required patrols of the Barden Moor and Fell Access areas, including the popular footpath routes to the summit of Simon's Seat. This became the start of the National Park's extremely successful voluntary service, the team of dedicated men and women who now contribute so much to the successful work of the National Park Authority.

Wilf, a naturally good communicator, was quick to realise the Warden Service had a major educational role. Rather than just telling people where they could not walk, better by far to tell them where they could, by erecting signs and waymarks, and eventually producing the first printed leaflets to explain the work of the National Park.

The Warden was also there as someone for farmers, who had bitterly opposed the National Park, to talk to. Initially he was seen as an official to complain or grumble to, gradually came the recognition that the Warden was on their side, someone who could try and deal with problems, help to direct people onto the paths and trails, encouraging them not to drop litter, light fires or disturb livestock. Education and understanding of why the countryside needed to be looked after was the most effective form of prevention of trespass and damage. In effect the National Park's Information service was born.

The National Park Committee was quick to appreciate that they now had their man on the ground. In 1965 a small caravan was purchased to be parked at key car parks where the public could be intercepted, ideally before they started out on their day's walk. In 1968 the Committee took over the old Reading Room in the Tudor Manor House in Clapham village to become the first National Park Information Centre in the National Park with exhibitions, maps and displays.

The North Riding Committee were soon to follow suit. In 1964 Norman Crossley, a Bradford man who had worked in the Dales as a seed salesman, got the job from among 400 applicants. As he was to later recall:

"I ran things with a core of voluntary wardens – 50 at the start and I ended up with 300. They didn't get anything, not even their expenses. They did it for the love of the thing. It worked. It was a very, very friendly sort of set-up.

"I had no office. I had a desk in the planning department at Northallerton and at my own expense I did up what had been an old peat store at our cottage in Stalling Busk. I also had an air-raid siren I was supposed to take out on the Land Rover in the event of nuclear attack. I don't know who was supposed to hear it.

"One of the questions visitors asked was: 'Where can we go, and what is there to do?' I composed some walks and wrote them out. There were no information centres then. We took a card table to Aysgarth car park and handed the walks out. It was a bit primitive."

In 1973 the North Riding finally acquired their own Visitor Centre in some disused railway buildings on railway land near Aysgarth Falls, where a popular cafe was also opened. But Norman also recalled the almost universal hostility of the farming community in the Northern Dales which was to take many years to overcome.

Eventually both Wardens – now known as the Head Warden in the West Riding, but the Official Warden in the North Riding – were able to recruit assistants, three in the West Riding – Joe Shevelan, John Lockwood and Peter Wright, and one in the North Riding, Lawrence Barker. Between them these six were to create the core of what is now the National Park's Ranger service, and to win the respect of local farmers and landowners who gradually came to realise these were people on their side, who they could talk to, who would fix a gate, stile or broken wall, would get out with a group of volunteers to repair a path or waymark a trail, and do much to encourage young people to take a responsible and caring attitude to the Dales and its natural beauty.

Tom Stephenson stands next to Fred Willey MP (right) at the April 1965 launch of the Pennine Way on Malham Moor. (YPN)

What neither the legislators nor indeed the opponents of National Parks had fully realised is that Britain was going through a profound period of social and economic change. People had much more money in their pockets – Prime Minister Harold Macmillan's famous words in 1957 "most of our people have never had it so good" had powerful resonance, and this was even more true in the 1960s. They were to spend new wealth on material goods, but above all to enjoy far greater personal mobility – the emergence of mass motoring. With ever improving roads including the growing motorway network, millions of people now lived within an hour's drive of the Yorkshire Dales.

They did not come to the Yorkshire Dales because it was a National Park. Only a minority knew or cared what a National Park was. They came because

it was Malham, Bolton Abbey, Ingleborough, Grassington, Aysgarth Falls. On Bank Holidays roads were jammed, car parks overflowing, riversides crowded with picnics, pubs and cafes heaving. Visitor numbers soared.

The new Yorkshire Dales National Park, divided into two, underfunded and its two Committees' time largely dominated by development control matters, with tiny numbers of staff on the ground, was overwhelmed on fine weekends and holiday periods.

There were some positive developments. Prime among these was the great survey of Public Rights of Way required by the 1949 Act and carried out by the two local authorities, recording every footpath, bridleway or byway. After a series of painstaking Public Inquiries, including examination at Draft and Provisional stages, these were finally recorded onto

The increase in popularity of walking in the Dales has led to a need to improve the rights of way network. This path to the summit of Whernside, used by an estimated 50,000 walkers per year, forms part of 27 kilometres of new footpath built by the National Park's innovative Three Peaks Project team to deal with the wear and tear resulting from this level of usage - see page 80. (Author)

a Definitive Map of Rights of Way. This process continued into the 1970s, and produced a superb network of walking, riding and off road cycling routes (and some off road motoring routes) that were to form the core of the outdoor enjoyment potential of the new National Park.

This also included key sections of Britain's first Long Distance Footpath, the Pennine Way, the vision of one man, Tom Stephenson, who having set out this vision in a newspaper feature in the *Daily Herald* in 1936, finally helped secure the necessary legislation in 1949. After years of tough negotiation, the Pennine Way was finally inaugurated on Malham Moor in 1965.

Significantly the Youth Hostel at Malham opened in 1938 to the designs of John Dower (and now known as the John Dower Memorial Hostel) was already there to welcome Pennine Way walkers, to be joined by a new hostel at Hawes, one of the first in the UK to be specifically built to serve walkers on a long distance path - the Pennine Way.

By the 1960s attitudes were changing. In 1962 the West Riding County Planning Office, supported by the West Riding Committee and the Joint Advisory

Limestone quarries were a major source of pollution in the early days of the National Park. Here is Swinden Quarry at its worst when the main road from Skipton to Grassington still ran through the middle of the plant. Heavy lorry traffic was a constant problem and it took many years before much of the output was switched to rail. (John S Murray)

Committee, took forward a proposal to extend the National Park into both the Forest of Bowland and Upper Nidderdale, even considering taking in the boundary from Bowland into neighbouring parts of Lancashire. Predictably there was strong opposition against any such proposals from District Councils and local politicians in both areas, and the idea was quietly dropped. The Forest of Bowland became a designated Area of Outstanding Natural Beauty in 1964 and Nidderdale was eventually to follow in 1990.

One reason which lay behind this thinking was to have a valuable long term impact on traffic and transport planning for the Yorkshire Dales and this was the concept of a Motorway/Trunk Road Box around the National Park – and the two eventual AONBs – to carry through traffic north and south, or east and west. This consisted of the M6 to the west, the A1(M), the A5/A59 to the south and the A66 to the north, with an avoidance of major through routes through the National Park. This has been a concept idea which has continuing resonance in the Dales in terms of resisting major highway improvement schemes to ensure that heavy through traffic avoids the protected landscapes.

Another major West Riding inspired project sadly failed to be realised. By the mid-1960s it was recognised that the huge development and expansion of limestone quarries in Ribblesdale and Upper Wharfedale was a major source of pollution and nuisance in the National Park. This was the development of a rail-based transit system to get bulk limestone taken out of the Dales by rail, with the building of a large transhipment centre in the Brighouse area, fed by improved siding facilities at both Swinden quarry and Horton quarries. By having a distribution system close to the M62, it was believed that not only bulk haul of limestone could be switched to rail, but smaller consignments could be taken away from the Dales by rail for transhipment onto lorries closer to their ultimate destination, thereby taking many thousands of tonne miles of heavy wagons away from Dales roads, with consequent reduction in noise, pollution and accident risk.

Sadly after local Government reorganisation in 1974, with the splitting up of the old West Riding into West Yorkshire and part of North Yorkshire, there was no longer a unified planning authority nor the political will to take the proposals forward. It took many more years to get a significant switch of heavy quarry traffic away from road to rail in the Dales, a process that is still under way.

The other major threat facing the special landscape of the Yorkshire Dales during the 1960s and early 1970s was heavily subsided monoculture afforestation. At this time generous tax concessions were available to landowners for the purpose of investment in forestry, allegedly in the national interest to restore 'reserves' of commercial softwood timber for pit props, paper making and the like and to save currency reserves, even though it was far more economical to plant, grow and harvest timber for example in the huge (renewable) forests of Scandinavia.

It soon became a popular way for industrialists, speculators and newly wealthy pop stars to keep their wealth out of the hands of the tax man until such time as the timber could be harvested. Environmentalists saw this rather differently. Huge areas of dark conifers in rectangular blocks changed the landscape. Once trees matured they produced dark, dense undercover where little wildlife could flourish – though for some species such as red squirrels, larch and spruce forests represent a good habitat. But the landscape loss was immense.

After much debate both Planning Committees began to take a strong line against such developments, and a Forestry Map was prepared to indicate areas where forestry schemes would be acceptable and where not. But another powerful player was about to enter the field. This was the North Pennines Rural Development Board, set up by the Wilson Government in 1969 as a way of stimulating and supporting the economic development of the Pennine uplands, between the Peak District and the Scottish Border, and covering most of the Yorkshire Dales. The new body had access to significant Government funds to help support the infrastructure of the area, including support for rural transport services (help was given to retain the bus services in Swaledale), giving grants for farming and forestry projects, including, controversially perhaps, support for the amalgamation of small upland farms into larger, more 'economic' units.

But when it was discovered that the Development Board could overrule the Park Committees over major forestry schemes, there was uproar. The problems focused on huge projects on open land at Greenfield above Langstrothdale, between upper Wharfedale and Ribblesdale. It was feared that these Development Board projects would only be the first of many other similar schemes which could totally change the landscape of the National Park, transforming it into something akin to the vast Kielder Forest in Northumberland, obliterating characteristic and historic landscape features, and removing access. Letters were written to the press. One issue raised by objectors was the problems that would occur 40 years later when timber had to be extracted in huge wagons along totally inadequate tracks and minor roads. This prediction has proved painfully true.

The battle was unsuccessful. Despite all the protests, the Development Board went ahead with the scheme. A landscape designer was employed to make a few cosmetic changes to reduce the visual impact.

In 1971, soon after the election of the incoming Heath Government, the abolition of the Rural Development Board was announced. Despite its potential to help the rural economy, the Board had made few friends. But the war against mass monoculture plantation in the Dales was not won. Within a few years there was a further major scheme to plant a huge forest along the shoulders of Cam Fell, adjacent to Greenfield Forest, even obliterating part of the Dales Way. Popular opposition against the 'serried ranks' of conifers came from no less a figure than the writer J.B.Priestley with a trenchant letter to *The Times*. Despite this protest the scheme went ahead, but a later project in 1978 to cover a further 300 acres of land at South House Moor on the shoulders of Ingleborough was finally defeated after vigorous campaigning.

But not long afterwards, realising that commercial monoculture afforestation was now being used merely as a tax avoidance scheme, the concessions on forestry investment were abolished and the threat of mass afforestation of the Dales disappeared overnight.

By the 1970s perceptions about man's relationship with the planet were changing. Conservation was a word on everyone's lips. The influential Club of Rome – a seemingly contradictory group of industrialists and ecological thinkers – produced a report suggesting that many of the world's key resources, including minerals, fuel and energy, could soon begin to run short. Pressures of population were threatening the world's most fragile eco-systems. Friends of the Earth was established as a pressure group in the UK in 1971. National Parks were seen to be part of an essential need to protect our precious environment. Governments now felt they had to respond.

Campaigners soon therefore had an even more important victory to celebrate. After much deliberation, and even a Royal Commission led by Lord Redcliffe-Maud (which was largely ignored by Government), radical new proposals to transform the structure of local Government were suggested. These came into being in 1974. The two historic counties of North and West Riding were abolished and replaced with the two Metropolitan Councils, West and South Yorkshire, and a huge new expanded version of the North Riding known as North Yorkshire, to incorporate most of the former rural areas of the West Riding in Craven and Harrogate, and (for a time) the city of York, into a new County of North Yorkshire, with three parishes in the north west of the National Park, Dent, Garsdale and Sedbergh, passing into Cumbria.

National Park campaigners saw this as an opportunity to secure the major changes they had worked for two decades to achieve, and that was to create properly funded, properly administered, independent National Parks, with their own staff and resources.

They almost succeeded. The 1972 Local Government Act required County Councils to

Objectors to blanket afforestation schemes in the 1960s rightly prophesied that extraction of the timber would ultimately be a major problem. This new track has had to be built through the serried ranks of conifers at Snaizeholme, Upper Wensleydale. (Author)

establish single committees for each National Park (apart from the two that already had Boards), but also required these Committees to employ a National Park Officer and to deliver a National Park Plan. They would carry out development control, forward planning and wider countryside duties, but a major breakthrough was that seventy-five per cent of their expenditure would now come directly from the National Exchequer through the National Park Supplementary Grant. Twenty-five per cent still came from local authorities, but this would also be subject to a rate support mechanism for rural authorities. So the 'lion's share' of funding would now come from central Government, not local ratepayers. This was a great improvement and did much to reduce local concerns.

But the new National Park Committee was still only a Committee under the ultimate control of the new North Yorkshire County Council. At least in its early years this would continue to be dominated by the officers and members of the former North Riding County Council, most of whom had more

sympathy with local farmers and landowners rather than urban visitors, many of whom were now living in what were the new Metropolitan Counties of West and South Yorkshire. At least in the days of the old West Riding County Council, people living in the West Riding towns and cities, working in the great manufacturing and mining industries which were the bedrock of England's prosperity, had a democratic voice, through their elected members on the West Riding Committee, about how the National Park on their doorstep, in their own county, was managed and what its priorities should be.

So whilst this was indeed a breakthrough in terms of the Yorkshire Dales National Park having its own officer and dedicated staff team, and at last the Park had been given, by central Government, reasonable resources to cope with the increasing demands, there was still potential for conflict. Such a conflict – which was to have long-term implications for all UK National Parks – was to occur within a short time in the life of the new committee.

Chapter Three

The National Park Comes of Age

On April 1st 1974 – amidst the usual jokes about All Fools' Day – the newly formed and unified Yorkshire Dales National Park Committee took control of what until then had been an embryonic, but fatally divided, National Park.

The committee was a carefully balanced mixture of 18 elected members representing North Yorkshire and Cumbria County Councils, with representatives of the three new District Councils (Craven, Richmondshire and South Lakeland) plus six people nominated by the Secretary of State through its advisory body, the Countryside Commission (the former National Parks Commission given a new and wider remit).

The new committee had already been meeting as a 'shadow' body in the rather grand surroundings of Northallerton County Hall, for some months before it finally took office in 1974. North Yorkshire County Council still provided key legal and financial advice and some administrative support for the new body.

Though technically a committee of the equally new North Yorkshire County Council, most members, especially the Minister's appointed members, saw their role as fulfilling a national responsibility, helping to look after an area which Parliament had decided was worthy of national protection.

The committee soon appointed their first Chairman, Keith Lockyer, a dental surgeon, local property developer and County Councillor from Grassington, who was soon to impose his vision of an energetic young organisation on to his fellow colleagues on the committee.

The next urgent task was to appoint their new National Park Officer, Richard Harvey, a young yet already senior planning officer from Somerset County Council, but originally from South Yorkshire. In the following months Richard was able to recruit a dynamic young team of professionals, able to bring a wide range of skills to the new organisation, not just planners, but people with experience in countryside interpretation, education, ecology and archaeology.

Key among first recruits to the new body were in fact the original team of National Park Wardens, now working for a unified National Park, Wilf Proctor now switching roles to become the Park's first Information Officer, with John Lockwood promoted to Head Warden. The Wardens were soon to be joined by a team of Field Assistants, capable of bringing many of the practical skills needed to repair the stiles and walls, erect signposts and deal with much of the day to day work of the growing National Park.

However, a key problem was where the headquarters of the Park should be situated. For the first few weeks of his appointment, Richard Harvey operated out of a small office in Thornborough Hall, Leyburn, with just one secretary. But once staff were recruited, finding new premises was urgent. As had been predicted, the former North and West Riding sections of the National Park were divided by a high moorland watershed and there was no central point where communications were easy or suitable buildings existed.

In the event, an opportunity emerged in Grassington where the fine house of 'Colvend', once known as Prospect House and home of the Duke of Devonshire's chief agent for the Grassington Moor Mines, had been purchased by West Riding County Council in 1973. This was primarily in order to acquire part of its adjacent land for a badly needed new village car park. Rather than selling the house off, North Yorkshire County Council, its new owner, were persuaded to have it converted to office premises for the new National Park Committee.

But that led to some debate about the need to have an effective presence in the northern area of the Park. Nor was there sufficient room to house all the proposed staff in that one building. After much debate and search, a property at Yorebridge House, next to the River Ure in Bainbridge was acquired, and converted to offices.

Whilst not an ideal arrangement, at least it gave a semblance of balance between the Richmondshire and Craven sides of the National Park. This was soon to assume a functional split, with Development Control in the northern side of the Park together with Forward Planning and specialist policy teams dealing with such matters as the soon to be designated village Conservation Areas, archaeology and ecology, being in the Bainbridge office. Development Control for Craven, plus what was loosely termed 'Field Services' – Wardens, information and related technical services, were based in Grassington.

Two young but capable Assistant National Park Officers were appointed, both former rising stars within the old North Riding – George Hallas who was to look after the Bainbridge Office and forward planning team and John Baker who was to be in charge of the Grassington office where the field service staff were based.

Bainbridge became – and remains though in a new purpose-designed building – headquarters of the National Park, where Richard Harvey had his office. Inevitably these arrangements were not ideal. Meetings between staff required a journey over high moorland roads, often impassable in winter. Two offices inevitably created their own dynamic, with a focus on forward planning and policy in the north – sometimes unkindly dubbed the 'University of Bainbridge' – whilst the south was more about making things happen on the ground in terms of looking after visitors, whether creating new exhibits for a visitor centre, researching a leaflet or repairing a footbridge or stile.

In reality they were two sides of the same coin.

Policies set the objectives, the directions, what needed to be achieved, the priorities. The field teams were about delivering those priorities. But central to both offices was Development Control, often the toughest task of all in a National Park, where officers had to implement policies which sounded fine in theory but when it came to taking tough decisions about people's lives, livelihoods and aspirations, could lead to stressful situations. Officers had to be objective in an area where personal opinion and prejudice could quickly lead to loss of patience.

Development Control remains, and probably will always remain, a controversial issue. Any organisation that appears to have power over how people use their own land and property is going to be resented. In fact the National Park has an outstanding record in terms of not only approving a significant majority of planning applications (a fact which reflects the positive and helpful advice given by planning officers to applicants to enable them to submit plans likely be approved), but doing so in well within the statutory recommended time period.

Things do go wrong. Sometimes the case for or against an application is finely balanced and the argument that application is against Policy Y or Policy Z may be of no consolation to the applicants whose plans are rejected. Sometimes for good or for ill, officers' recommendations are overturned by Planning Committee members, as they have a democratic right to do, but not necessarily for the best or most open reasons. Other times planning mistakes are made and the consequences have to be lived with. At times in the past officers could be high handed and there are always anecdotes to be heard in any Dales pub about delays, prevarication, or decisions which have gone wrong. Some local people believe that planning itself is some kind of anti-democratic plot. But the truth is that contrary to sometimes emotional outbursts, for most – but of course not all – of the time the planners get it right. When planning goes smoothly and well, it doesn't tend to get discussed in the local pub.

Likewise forward planning in terms of both the Local Plan and Management Plans which for most people are abstract and remote from their day to day concerns. There is also an inevitable weakness among every local planning body that has existed, that imagines that as long as there is an approved Plan and a Designation in a report in a file then the job is done. It isn't. Merely giving something an acronym label such as SSSIs, SCA or SPA in a planning document doesn't actually change anything on the ground if action is not taken to protect the habitat or natural feature in question.

As someone rightly said, when the officers and committee get it right, people don't notice, because the landscape looks unchanged, so planners don't get the credit. The new development looks as if it has always been there. When they get it wrong, you suffer an eyesore that everyone has to live with. No matter how carefully and cleverly guidelines are drawn, there is always a subjective element to decision taking over Development Control issues and this has always been, and remains, a problem for the National Park.

Nevertheless, the real test of the success of the National Park is the degree to which the distinctive character of so many lovely stone-built villages has been retained. Most reasonable people would agree that by and large, over the sixty years of its existence, the officers and Planning Committees of the National Park have done a great job. There are, inevitably, a few exceptions, but generally the system has worked remarkably well. It does not take a great deal of imagination to think what the Dales – especially the southern areas within easy commuting distance of Leeds, Bradford, Harrogate, Burnley or even Manchester – would be like if there had been unrestricted building and road development over the last 60 years.

But this idea has not proved popular with many people in the local community, and over the decades many local politicians have seen it as an easy way to get support on election day to feed on these prejudices by attacking the National Park in the local press as some kind of alien, undemocratic body determined to stop local people making a living or interfering with their way of life.

Nothing could be further from the truth. In fact not only are planning applications dealt with more quickly in the Yorkshire Dales than by planning departments in many neighbouring authorities, but a higher proportion get eventual approval, often due to the careful advice given by officers to ensure that applicants 'get it right' in terms of visual appeal and quality of construction work. If this, inevitably, causes development to be more expensive than in outside areas in terms of high design standards and construction materials, this is ultimately a factor which has to be faced, though it also means support needs to be given to help people who need affordable housing. The Yorkshire Dales are, after all, a special place.

The new committee soon had much to be proud of. Soon at least some of the negative attitudes began slowly to disappear as there was greater understanding of what the National Park was actually about. Farmers might still grumble about the planners, but the much increased presence of the Warden Service on their land, together with field assistants, all local men and eventually women who were part of the community (it took some time before the Park eventually appointed its first female Ranger, as Wardens are now known) helped to change attitudes. Well repaired stiles with clear way-marked paths and signs reduce trespass and damage, especially through enclosed fields, and there was grudging acceptance that imaginatively produced exhibitions and displays were doing a lot of good to help people who had been brought up in urban environments to understand what hill farming and upland conservation was about. Leaflets of recommended walks kept people onto the more robust footpaths and emphasised the need for considerate behaviour, and National Park guided walks, led by the growing team of experienced volunteers, were also a very cost effective way of teaching people about the countryside and the need for responsible attitudes.

Plans were developed to create greater awareness of wider environmental issues. This included producing regular publications aimed at both locals and visitors, highlighting the many activities and achievements. Gradually the National Park was beginning to understand the need for good public

Hawes station, photographed shortly after closure in 1964. Much of it was later incorporated into the new Dales Countryside Museum. (D Hardy)

relations and that it was as important to get their message across to all stakeholders, be they visitors, the local community, farmers or landowners, or other land managers and public and private agencies.

A fine new purpose-built Information Centre – soon to be renamed a National Park Centre – was opened in Malham in 1975, to be followed by one at Hawes in the old Railway Station warehouse where in later years it was to form part of the fine Dales Countryside Museum, housing the nationally important collection of Dales farming and domestic artefacts collected by the remarkable Dales historians, collectors and authors, Marie Hartley and Joan Ingilby. Other Centres followed at Sedbergh in an old shop in Joss Lane, in a purpose-designed building in Grassington car park, and at Reeth also in a small former shop on the village green. The National Park was now in business.

Even in the early days there were still problems

with the parent County Council. As early as 1975 the Park Committee took a decision to prioritise the maintenance and improvement of its superb footpaths and bridleway network as key to understanding and discovering. Only a few years previously the Definitive Maps for the Dales had been completed and the Ordnance Survey were publishing the first maps with this vital new information – at first on 1:50,000 scale Landranger maps to be followed by the larger scale 1:25,000 green Pathfinder, later to become the larger and popular Outdoor Leisure Maps.

But by the mid-1970s, many paths were in a poor state of repair, and often difficult to follow with blocked stiles and wired up gates. There were even some serious inaccuracies and drafting mistakes with paths shown on the wrong side of walls or, as on Ingleborough summit, vanishing over a sheer cliff face.

Marie Hartley and Joan Ingilby, who donated their nationally important collection of farming and domestic artefacts to the Dales Countryside Museum. (Bertram Unné)

A top priority was to carry out a detailed survey of footpaths and bridleways and this was undertaken by volunteers and even Park staff in their spare time. It was clear from this survey that huge effort and resources were needed to allow the path network to become fit for purpose. It was realised that one problem was that the two highway authorities — North Yorkshire and Cumbria County Councils — had neither the resources nor the political will to spend more than the absolute minimum of time and money on footpaths, faced as they were with many other pressing demands on those resources for their road and highway maintenance programmes. To relieve NYCC and CCC of some of their problems and costs therefore seemed something that the National Park Committee might be able to do

Happily agreement was soon reached. Whilst the legal responsibility for the Definitive Map of Rights of Way was to remain with North Yorkshire and Cumbria County Councils, they were prepared to delegate maintenance work in the Park area to the National Park Committee. Field staff and volunteers could now begin to tackle the huge backlog of work to make the network useable for the growing numbers of walkers, who, armed with their shiny new maps, wanted to discover the footpath heritage.

But the committee also decided it needed further help with some of the complex technical aspects of rights of way, and therefore decided, with agreement from the Countryside Commission who were responsible for most of the National Park's actual funding, to put the appointment of a Footpath

Officer in their 1976/7 budget.

At the same time, the Park Committee were asked to provide a rescue operation for Britain's first Caving Centre at Whernside Manor in Dentdale, at that time owned by the Scouts Association. As the Yorkshire Dales is one of the leading UK centres for caving and potholing, the committee decided that Whernside Manor, a Georgian House in its own grounds, should be acquired to ensure its continuation and to develop it as a centre of excellence for caving, speleology and outdoor education generally. Funds were identified, including external grants, and budgets were approved.

However the National Park's budgets all had to be finally approved, before any expenditure could be made, by the Finance and Resources Committee of the North Yorkshire County Council. To the dismay of the National Park Committee, the NYCC Committee refused to approve the expenditure. As was pointed out, Whernside Manor wasn't even in North Yorkshire and there then followed some heated debate leading to a rebellion by the appointed members of the Park Committee, supported by the Chairman. So in spring 1976 a delegation of the Chairman, the National Park Officer and three appointed members travelled to London to seek a meeting with the Secretary of State for the Environment, in effect to complain about the interference by the County Council in the decision making of the National Park.

Although the Minister refused to directly intervene, there is little doubt that behind the scenes the rebellion had a major impact. Pressure on the County Council via the Countryside Commission, the Government's advisors, led to decisions being reversed. Whernside Manor was duly purchased in 1977 to become the National Caving Centre (sadly since closed) and the Footpath Officer was appointed.

From that time of rebellion, relations between the two bodies gradually improved, but there is little doubt that these events were instrumental in future radical changes to National Park administration.

The Yorkshire Dales was one of the first UK National Parks to take control of the management of its footpath and bridleway networks from their local authorities. The superb state of footpaths in the Yorkshire Dales has been one of the Park's great success stories. As relationships improved, the Park also worked closely with the County Council's legal officers in a variety of projects to modify the right of way network, not to 'rationalise' the footpath network as ramblers had feared, but to seek agreements with ramblers and farmers to remove anomalies and in some cases improve the path network, to make it better for walkers and landowners alike. Many of the most popular footpaths in Malham for example, between Malham Cove and Gordale Scar, were improved in this way in the late 1970s, though most walkers now assume these are ancient paths which have been there for centuries.

County Council interference and Forestry issues – most notably Cam Fell – and a feeling that the National Park was too dominated by pro-development factions within the Dales who were quick to criticise it in the local press for personal political advantage, led to a small group of people living in the Park to decide that conservation needed a stronger voice. After meetings in various people's homes, in October 1981 the first formal meeting of the Yorkshire Dales Society took place with a visit to a hill farm at Buckden in Upper Wharfedale.

The concept behind the society was initially to give an effective voice to the many local residents who wanted to ensure that the National Park did its job to protect the special landscape and distinctive culture of the Dales. They felt that the National Park was not doing enough to get its message across strongly enough to the wider local community. Many elected members too often only listened to vocal local business and development interests when it came to taking important decisions. Such people did not represent the majority even of local opinion, nor did they represent the views of the millions of visitors who came to the Dales. There was risk of the National Park becoming too parochial.

However the society was also among the first voluntary organisations to recognise the vital importance of the local hill farming community who were key to protecting the landscape. If this was indeed a cultural landscape shaped by generations of working farmers, foresters, estate managers and skilled artisans who had worked the land, planted the trees, built the walls, barns and farmhouses, a healthy, vibrant local economy was essential to maintain and keep that same distinctive and special landscape. The mantra 'a landscape is a people' became a key part of what the Society was, and remains, faithful to, and this was long before later changes in legislation that gave Park Authorities powers to be involved with local social and economic issues.

With local support from CPRE and the Ramblers Association, and from several existing and former appointed members of the National Park Committee, and with backing from both the Countryside Commission and the Council for National Parks, the organisation grew rapidly and within a couple of years soon had over 1,000 members, many of them people living and working in the Dales. Among founder members were Arthur Raistrick, Arthur Dower, Pauline Dower and Graham Watson, retired mill owner later to give his huge Upper Wharfedale Estate to the National Trust in memory of his brother. In its early years, the YDS was based in Grassington, its first chairman being the former Chairman of the National Park Committee, Keith Lockyer.

The society soon saw itself as the 'critical friend' of the National Park, able and willing to speak out on issues, such as the extension of quarrying permissions where it felt the Park was not doing what it should be doing in putting its prime purpose to support conservation and protection of the landscape first. The YDS's very presence acts as an important counter-weight to powerful local development and commercial interests, and sees itself as the 'conscience' of the National Park.

After some initial unease about the role of the new body, the relationship between the Park and the society has been a cordial one, but there continue to be occasions where the society will speak out when and where it feels the National Park Authority is not delivering on key issues, be they linked to developmental control matters or wider Park management issues.

But a major step change in the history of the National Park was to come in 1997 when the measures of the 1995 Environment Act were finally implemented. This important piece of legislation established fully independent, properly funded National Park Authorities. This meant that the National Park was no longer a Committee of the Council, but an National Park Authority responsible for its own administration, finances and legal services, a truly independent Board as envisaged in the 1949 Act. It was soon able to move to its own new purpose-built, low carbon headquarters at Yoredale House in Bainbridge.

As well as achieving standards of excellence in terms of its visitor management, including one of the best maintained and signed networks of footpaths and bridleways in any UK National Park, there was major progress in communicating the National Park's message through a range of high quality publications, press and PR activities using professional journalists so that local communities and visitors alike understood the Park's work. Far better resourced interpretation and educational services encouraged greater understanding of the unique and special environment of the National Park. There were also new outreach services, with professional staff and volunteers working with local schools and also with schools and groups in the catchment cities in and around the National Park. These included ethnic minority groups, working with the Campaign for National Park's Mosaic Partnership to encourage people from ethnic minority backgrounds to enjoy and experience the National Park. Such work brought new audiences to help achieve greater understanding and enjoyment of what the Park was about, that key second purpose.

A recent example of just such an initiative has been the *Go Dales* project. This was designed to create awareness and broaden the National Park's appeal to younger, more active visitors, especially younger females. Launched in 2008 and supported by Sport England, and other partners, *Go Dales* was targeted at young people between the ages of 8 and 25 living

The footpath to Malham Cove in 1974. Erosion problems were already evident with walkers often avoiding the path itself as seen here. (Telegraph & Argus)

Improvements to the path in the late 1970s may have created what has been unkindly described as a pedestrian motorway, but at least they help to cope with extreme visitor pressure and discourage users from constantly trampling the grass. (Bruce Rollinson – YPN)

The huge Upper Wharfedale Estate was given to the National Trust by retired mill owner Graham Watson. It includes much of the magnificent limestone scenery of Langstrothdale, which has this tiny settlement of Yockenthwaite in its midst. (Jim Moran – YPN)

in towns and cities within an hour's travel time of the National Park. It attracted several hundred participants who were given an introduction to a range of activities within the special environment of the National Park such as caving, climbing, sailing, horse riding, geocaching, hill walking, canoeing and mountain biking.

A clear mission of the new independent Authority was its wide commitment on the issue of sustainability. This has since become an overused word, but was originally based on the seminal report of the Brundtland Commission – *The World Commission on Environment and Development* – of 1987. This report recognised the need for industrial development in the world to exist within parameters of what the environment could, in the longer term, 'sustain' in terms of human pressure on vulnerable eco systems, and the need to avoid damaging over-exploitation of the world's resources, whether land or ocean based, upon which humanity must ultimately depend for its survival. National Parks clearly have a key role in such development, as areas where new ideas about the future management of land and resources could be tested – what the late Malcolm McEwan described in 1981 as 'Greenprints for the Future'.

Sustainability was a concept that ran through all the work of the Authority for the next couple of decades, including eventually adoption of its own energy saving measures so that it would be, as much as any public authority could be, carbon neutral. But this was equally true in other areas of work, including the Park's own visitor management work. This approach was spearheaded by the Authority's Deputy Park Officer, John Baker, who tragically was to die prematurely in 1998, his memory fittingly recalled by the John Baker exhibition and teaching room in the Hawes Countryside Museum, but even more famously by the remarkable story of the fundraising calendar which has raised over £1.3 million for Leukaemia Research and became a hugely successful film – *The Calendar Girls*.

The Environment Act 1995 also added a new power (as opposed to duty) and that was Park Authorities, in pursuing their core duties of conservation and enjoyment, should 'seek to foster the economic and social wellbeing' of local communities within the National Park but 'without incurring any significant expenditure in so doing' and working in co-operation with other authorities.

There has been much debate into the precise meaning of these words, but for the first time Park Authorities were required to 'seek to' help local communities as a by-product of their other activities. This was to have particular importance in terms of the work of the National Park Authority in such areas as rural tourism and outdoor activity projects, linked to issues such as rural leisure transport, though key areas such as housing, social care, education and transport for local communities remained firmly with the local authorities.

But a sudden, catastrophic event was to overtake the Yorkshire Dales and give the Authority reason to use its new social and economic powers: Foot and Mouth disease. The terrible outbreak in 2001-2 which led to the massive tragic slaughter of thousands of sheep and cattle, devastating many hill farming communities, was to have a profound and lasting impact on the Dales with much personal distress and hardship among farmers. One perhaps unforeseen outcome was the massive loss of visitor income, when, with the closure of all footpaths and bridleways, the millions of visitors who used to arrive each year to enjoy the walking, climbing and riding opportunities of the National Park no longer came in the summer of 2001. The impact on many Dales businesses, not just tourism business, but on shops, garages, cafes, pubs and their suppliers and service providers, was profound. Much of the economy of the Dales collapsed. Many businesses didn't recover and folded, others struggled to survive.

Even after the paths were reopened, visitors were slow to return – having discovered other areas whist the Dales were closed, including new walking areas outside Britain, elsewhere in Europe such as Majorca or Southern Spain. New offers of budget flights and cheaper accommodation, as well as year-round sunny weather, proved powerful alternatives for many walkers who had been unwilling to visit the Dales in the 18 months or so during which off-tarmac access to the National Park had been closed.

The realisation that visitors were not just nuisances to be 'managed' in terms of reducing footpath erosion and traffic congestion, but the economic lifeblood of the area, changed attitudes within the National Park profoundly. Visitors, especially walkers, were so crucial economically, and could no longer be treated with snobbish disdain.

However it was also recognised that if the Brundtland concept of Sustainable Development was central to balancing the many pressures on the environment with economic realities, tourism in the fragile environment of the National Park had to be of a scale and nature to meet principles. Sustainable Tourism therefore meant tourism which inflicted least harm on the environment or on local communities whilst delivering the maximum local economic benefit. Two core activities in the Yorkshire Dales, walking and cycling, were now seen to be not only superb ways of understanding and appreciating the rich cultural and natural heritage of the Dales, but the longer visitors stayed – especially if they spent one night or more in the area – the more money they spent. Moreover as many economists point out, this money generally stays in the area as an 'economic multiplier' – the bed and breakfast provider would buy bacon and bread from the local grocer or baker, who in turn might source at least some goods such as milk and eggs from local farms or other suppliers.

Popular long distance trails such as the Pennine Way, the Dales Way and Wainwright's Coast to Coast bring staying visitors and their spending power into the area. What the terrible Foot and Mouth epidemic ironically achieved therefore, was realisation that the National Park should be actively involved in supporting such activity, tying in with the new social and economic purposes. Given the increasing recognition of the health value of outdoor recreation, National Parks could now be seen as promoting both sustainable economic growth, and physical and mental wellbeing to the wider community.

This was given huge impetus with the passing of the Countryside and Rights of Way Act in 2000, usually shortened to the more memorable CROW Act. If its implementation was delayed because of Foot and Mouth, the National Park Authority was soon able to work closely with the Countryside Agency to establish a highly ambitious programme of work with farmers, landowners, managers and user groups. This work was supported by the Dales Access Forum, a key stakeholder and user group, established in 2002. A key task was to establish which of the many areas of unenclosed countryside met the criteria of Open Countryside to be designated Access Land under the Act, as well as dealing with many other aspects of rights of way and access legislation, a process which continues.

It was a herculean task, but by 2005 the Dales was officially declared 'open' in terms of public access. Whereas prior to 2005 only four per cent of the land in the Yorkshire Dales National Park had official legal public access to open land, in 2005 this shot up to sixty-two per cent, a massive 390 square miles of open access. This was the most dramatic change to access availability on open land in any National Park in the United Kingdom.

Open access did not mean the 'free for all' or 'Right to Roam' that many landowners feared. There were quite strict rules. Certain areas of land management or ecological areas were not opened up. Dogs – a major worry for landowners and estate managers – could be banned. Moors could be closed at times on an agreed number of days of the year when shooting was to take place, and at time of high fire risk. In fact compared with the old unregulated 'de facto' access, the new CROW Act brought in a greater degree of control and regulation.

In truth, most walkers don't wish to walk far from a clear path or track. The demand among walkers to walk the wild places is small. But the right to do so if they wish is perhaps deeply symbolic, a cherished freedom. The fears of landowners about 'hoards' of walkers tramping the heather, scaring the grouse chicks, knocking down walls and leaving huge amounts of litter and damage, were largely unfounded. But clear maps (open access land now appears on all larger scale OS maps) and well signed access and entry points to open moorland has made life much easier for walkers, though there are still

Celebrating the opening of the new CROW Act Public Access Areas in the Yorkshire Dales in 2005. (Author)

Educational work forms a key role for the Yorkshire Dales Millennium Trust. Tom Ducket developed his skills under the Dales Countryside Trainee Scheme and is seen busy repairing a drystone wall on the Ingleborough National Nature Reserve. (Natural England)

The Yorkshire Dales Millennium Trust has played a leading role in working with disadvantaged groups from nearby catchment towns and cities. These three photos show participants in its People and the Dales project.

A group from Keighley visits Catrigg Foss, near Settle. (Judy Rogers – YDMT)

Tree planting in Wharfe, near Austwick, was undertaken by Laisterdyke College. (Judy Rogers – YDMT)

Anna Autiero, group leader for Bradford Action for Refugees, on a training session in Malham. (Gail Smith – YDMT)

places where literally it is not possible to get onto open moorland without trespass or climbing walls.

Despite the many huge improvements to the human and financial resources available to the National Park Authority, it was always clear that there would never be enough money to achieve all that was needed. The Authority realised, too, that it was only one player in the game. As well as the farmers, estate mangers and landowners that the Authority needed to work with, there were other key players with often far greater resources than the National Park yet who shared many of the same objectives – bodies such as the Countryside Agency and English Nature, (in 2006 combined into Natural England), the Environment Agency, the Forestry Commission and the new Water Companies who still have statutory duties over the land they managed. By working in partnership with these organisations, far more could be achieved than by the Authority working in isolation.

But how could a public authority attract new funding at a time of increasing public sector spending cuts? It was realised that there were still plenty of Government and private sector grants available to non-Government bodies, but how could this be used to benefit?

As Millennium year – 2000 – began to get closer, the National Park Authority realised that there could be major new funding available through the recently established Millennium Commission.

The solution was a highly imaginative one, led by the then Chairman of the Park Authority, Robert Heseltine, with the support of the National Park Officer Richard Harvey and his two Deputies, John Baker and George Hallas (who was later to take over from Richard as the Park's Chief Officer), and that was to set up the Yorkshire Dales Millennium Trust in 1996. Set up as a charity and not-for-profit Company Limited by Guarantee, its mission is 'to support the environmental, social and economic well-being of the Yorkshire Dales'. These objectives mirror many of those of the National Park, but with a strong emphasis on wider socio-economic issues in the Dales, to cover such matters as apprenticeships and training. But the Trust operates well outside the narrow confines of the National Park's boundaries, covering Nidderdale AONB and areas beyond into the Forest of Bowland. Its first Chairman was a local retired teacher from Hawes, Roger Stott, and the other Trustees were, and are, drawn from a wide variety of bodies. These include the Authority itself and supporting groups such as the Yorkshire Dales Society – who see it as a project delivery organisation in contrast to its more educational and campaigning role – CPRE, Country Landowners Association and Ramblers, but there are also several independent members noted for their work within their local communities, including for a time the Marquis of Hartington before he became the present Duke of Devonshire.

Early success came with the award of grants in 1997 for two major schemes, the *Environet* and *Dales Living Landscapes* project, which between them brought in £5.5 million of Lottery funds into the Dales. These had to be matched from locally raised funding from donations, legacies, grants from landowners, local business and other partners, but above all many thousands of smaller donations from the public, many gifted through a popular scheme to plant a tree in memory of a loved one in one of several Memorial Woodlands in the National Park.

But this was only the beginning. By 2008 over 700 projects worth £15 million had been developed in the Dales – including hundreds of tree planting and woodland restoration schemes, wildlife habitat protection, the restoration of hundreds of barns, drystone walls, village halls and historic buildings as well as hundreds of small scale village and environmental schemes.

A key part of YDMT's role is educational work with schemes for young people such as *Learning in Limestone Country* and the *Dales Countryside Trainee Scheme* designed to work with students in developing a range of countryside heritage skills. As a charity it has played a leading role in working with disadvantaged groups in the nearby catchment towns and cities, including such projects as *People and the Dales* helping people with learning and physical disabilities, from ethnic minorities, disadvantaged backgrounds and even with refugees, enabling them to experience and enjoy the life-enhancing experience of the wild open spaces of the Yorkshire Dales.

Another YDMT scheme focused on local communities was *Caring for the Parish*. This included the appointment of 'Parish Caretakers' to undertake small scale projects in village communities with a strong local environmental and heritage focus, such as creating meadows on village greens, managing verges, waymarking and signing local paths, putting up nest boxes, looking after churchyards, playgrounds and village halls.

Whilst the YDMT is totally independent from the Park Authority, from its initial Millennium Commission project funding, it has been able to secure continued funding within the Dales for a wide range of immensely important and worthwhile conservation and landscape projects which benefit the National Park and sites within the greater Dales area, including Nidderdale AONB. None of these would have been possible for the Park Authority to achieve on its own.

The Trust also has a small team of specialist staff under the guidance of its Director, David Sharrod, who work extremely closely with National Park staff on a variety of mainly practical conservation-led projects, or related work, for example with the administration of the National Park's own Sustainable Development Fund. The Trust's funding comes from a wide variety of sources – from donations, large and small, but also from a variety of grants which are accessible to charities, and above all from the management of environmental projects for other agencies in the Dales. This means that the Trust's staff are paid on a consultancy basis for their management time and expertise, which in turn helps to pay for the organisation's modest overheads. Though the Trust does not have any members as such, it has around 20,000 or so supporters, whose constant financial support and help, for example with small fund raising events and activities, enables the Trust to achieve its targets, often against the odds, at a time when external project funding is increasingly difficult to find. As key partners to the National Park Authority, the Trust has enabled many more of the Park's own most worthwhile policy objectives to be delivered in more concrete, practical ways than the Park Authority could have done within its own limited resources. By 2014, the Trust had delivered in its lifetime over 1,200 environmental projects with a total value of £20 million – all money spent in the local Dales economy – in and around the Yorkshire Dales.

In later chapters we touch on some of these achievements. The point to emphasise is that it was the vision of the National Park Authority, with initial financial backing and help in kind including staff resources, that enabled the Trust to be created. Once established, it has been able to deliver many hugely worthwhile and practical schemes, which the National Park as a public sector body and subject to all the usual constraints on expenditure, would not have been able to achieve.

It is a huge success story – and this success continues.

Chapter Four

Conserving the Barns and Hay Meadows

There are few lovelier sights in England than to stand on a hillside in Swaledale or Upper Wensleydale in late May or early June, to look across the landscape with its high brown fells enclosing the more sheltered green pastures, the intricate patterns of drystone walls and scattered stone barns leading into the flower rich meadows in the valley bottom, with their subtle mixture of greens, yellow, golds, pinks, even touches of purple. To walk through such meadows, keeping to the well-marked public paths, perhaps getting your boots dusted with pollen, is an unforgettable experience, a feeling of enjoying timeless beauty.

But what we are experiencing is in fact a landscape that reflects a particular kind of land management which flourished from medieval times up to around the 1950s. It was a truly sustainable form of livestock farming, one which fitted closely with the rhythm of the seasons and the natural productive capacity of the land. The meadows were mowed by hand each year to provide the rich crop of hay to be stored in the lofts of the outlying barns where cattle could be overwintered; the hay at one and the same time providing insulation in the coldest part of the Dales winter and essential feed for the cattle. The mucking out of the cattle fertilised the fields in early spring to provide another hay crop in the summer.

But it was also a highly labour intensive routine, requiring hard physical labour not only from the farming families themselves, but seasonal casual labour of hundreds of migrant farm workers from other parts of England or Ireland to cut and store the hay.

Rapid mechanisation of farms after World War II, plus the use of fast growing varieties of grass seed, chemical fertilisers to speed up growth and herbicides to rid the meadows of unwanted 'weeds' (or wild flowers if you saw them that way), not only allowed milk and beef production to increase in order to meet the growing markets of post-war, industrial England, but required a fraction of the scarce and by then expensive labour to achieve that higher productivity.

But this move to more efficient forms of farming and changes in the economics of hill farming also caused massive social and economic change, with many farms amalgamating to create more economically viable units. Many farming families were forced to leave the area, to be replaced by often more affluent incomers choosing to retire or have a second home in the Dales, and upgrade the old

The wonderful landscape of Swaledale with its intricate patterns of drystone walls and scattered stone barns. In early summer light there are few lovelier sights in England. (Robert White – YDNPA)

A similar scene in Wensleydale with barns and hay meadows again a dominant feature. (Bruce Rollinson – YPN]

A matchless photograph by Marie Hartley and Joan Ingilby from their classic book Life and Tradition in the Yorkshire Dales. Cherry Kearton and his horse Pat are using a sweep to bring hay down to a barn at Moor Close, Upper Swaledale.

farmhouses to standards and comforts that the original inhabitants could scarcely imagine.

This vanished world was brilliantly captured, just before it began to disappear, by the authors Marie Hartley and Joan Ingilby in their classic book *Life and Tradition in the Yorkshire Dales* published in 1968. Based on interviews with hundreds of Dales people who grew up and worked on farms in the years before mechanisation, the book gives an absorbing insight into what is a now forgotten way of life. This is also superbly illustrated by their magnificent collection of farming and domestic artefacts now displayed in the Dales Countryside Museum in Hawes.

But without its original economic purpose, much

of this historic, distinctive barns and walls landscape of the Yorkshire Dales, is also threatened with unwelcome decay. Whilst the farmhouses and farm workers' cottages enjoy a new lease of life in a more leisured society, the outlying barns have a less secure future. Most of the several thousand of surviving field barns date from between 1750 and 1850, and are superb examples of vernacular architecture in their own right. But many are now reaching an age when, without significant maintenance investment, roof beams sag and collapse, doors fall off their hinges, missing slates allow rainwater to penetrate, walls begin to crack and bulge.

A similar threat faces the estimated 8,000

Field barns are superb examples of domestic architecture in their own right. This survivor is near Hebden in Upper Wharfedale. (Alan Headlam)

Many barns in Swaledale and Arkengarthdale have been restored under a Conservation Area scheme, which has since been extended to other parts of the Dales. This example near Healaugh is seen being re-roofed and then later in what is described as its 'post-consolidation' state. (Robert White – YDNPA)

kilometres (5,000 miles) of drystone walls in the Yorkshire Dales National Park. Many follow ancient boundaries of ownership and date back to medieval times. Most were built in the last five hundred years enclosing small fields around farms, using locally quarried stone. There was a massive spate of wall building from the late 18th to the mid-19th century at the period of Parliamentary Enclosures of the open common lands, especially enclosure of the open high moorland, with long straight lines of walls crossing the fell sides and summits or following watersheds which are such a feature of the Dales landscape.

Though many of these boundary walls still have an important function, it is often cheaper and easier to replace them with ugly post and wire fences, often with barbed wire, whilst in the smaller enclosures, walls that no longer have a function are often left to collapse leaving an ugly line of scattered stone. Unless walls are

Vast lengths of drystone walls have been repaired in recent years, thus both improving the appearance of the landscape and contributing to the local economy. Stan Heywood is busily at work at Wharfe, near Austwick (Don Gamble – YDMT)

Bumblebee on a melancholy thistle. Maintaining traditional flower-rich meadows helps to foster bees and butterflies on which so much other wildlife depends. (Don Gamble – YDMT)

regularly maintained, and gaps, whether a result of sheep, rain, snow or even the occasional walker, quickly repaired, the gaps soon spread. Too often they are simply filled with makeshift corrugated iron or wire netting, and what was a fine landscape feature becomes scruffy or semi derelict in appearance. Most hill farmers no longer have the income, time, nor indeed the skilled labour available to maintain those walls and barns.

There was a realisation, even as far back as the 1970s, that the key to maintaining the beauty of the National Park meant working closely with landowners and farmers, supporting them, and helping them to maintain, for the wider public benefit, those very landscape features both they and the visiting public value so highly.

The concept of Upland Management soon took hold in many National Parks such as the Lake District, Dartmoor, the North York Moors and the Yorkshire Dales, whereby farmers would be helped by National Park Rangers and field staff to repair stiles and walls or to bring in contract labour to help. But in areas like the Dales, with thousands of barns and miles of walls to maintain, this required more than small-scale repair schemes, however welcome these were. There was growing recognition by the 1980s, that in both National Parks and Areas of Outstanding Natural Beauty, a more radical approach was needed.

Up until then nature conservation was seen as purely a site based activity – looking after plants and wildlife habitats in National or Local Nature Reserves, or employing stronger controls in the management of what were known as Sites of Special Scientific Interest. The 1981 Wildlife and Countryside Act had recognised the need to compensate farmers, whose land included an SSSI which prevented them from using modern farming methods, for example the heavy use of fertilisers, for loss of income. But it was soon realised that protection of wildlife in the National Park required more than a few protected sites, and a much more area-wide and holistic approach.

This resulted in a shift from the traditional forms of upland farming support schemes with 'headage'

payments based on numbers of sheep and cattle, an approach which could result in overgrazing, towards a system of support payments which also reflected Society's wider concerns for environmental and aesthetic goals. If we want to protect the natural world, wildlife habitats and magnificent countryside within which they exist, these are outputs as important as wool or beef production, and farmers who help to deliver this public benefit needed to be compensated accordingly. Farmers and land managers are the only true keepers of the countryside and need to be encouraged, supported, and ultimately rewarded for achieving goals which society may cherish but which, if they don't have an economic benefit for the farmer in terms of increased agricultural production, the public has to pay for.

Interestingly enough, the major initiative for change came from outside the UK, the European Union, which for the first time in 1985 recognised the many important environmental dimensions to farming. It was a much needed reform of the Common Agricultural Policy which, with its emphasis purely on food production, had produced unwanted food 'mountains', often at the cost of significant environmental damage in terms of overgrazing and degradation of soils and landscape features.

It was realised that the intervention by Governments and the EU in the farm payments system must therefore now have social and environmental as well as economic aims. This was first brought into UK legislation through the 1986 Agriculture Act which for the first time set up Environmentally Sensitive Areas (ESAs) in the uplands. Farmers within an ESA could enter into voluntary agreement with what is now DEFRA to help them maintain rather than merely exploit the countryside. The ESA had two main objectives – '*to maintain existing landscape, wildlife and historical features created by traditional farming methods and b) to re-creation of tradition features lost as result of modern farming methods*'.

The Pennine Dales ESA was established in 1985, and covered an area from Northumberland and the

North Pennines to most of the Yorkshire Dales. Outside the ESA similar Countryside Stewardship schemes were adopted. These schemes have all eventually been absorbed into Environmental Stewardship schemes at two levels, Entry, and Higher Level, each with differing levels of requirements and commitment to qualify for the payments.

A further intervention from the European Union to protect wildlife and wildlife habitats, including birds, through its Species and Habitats Directives are Special Protection Areas (SPAs) and Special Areas for Conservation (SACs) all of which form part of the Natura 200 sites of international importance. There are a number of such sites within the Yorkshire Dales. What is important about these designations is not the wealth of jargon and indeed the tiresome red tape attached to them, but the fact that this is a national commitment and obligation by Government to recognise these definitions and targets within its own policies, which have to be delivered at local level.

Payments to farmers and landowners are therefore subject to agreement with Natural England on such matters as the types and nature of fertilisers to use, maintaining stock proof walls and traditional features on the farm, and only mowing the hay crop when the flowers in herb-rich meadows have already seeded.

'Agri-environmental agreements', as they are now more generally known, offer farmers and landowners a complex system of carrots and stick, even covering such aspects of extra payments to change soil fertility to encourage certain species, or re-introduce a rare or threatened species of sheep. In the Yorkshire Dales National Park something like 85% of the Park is covered by such agreements. These include Entry Level and High Level Stewardship schemes – which in 2014 are due to be replaced by a new scheme under the Rural Development Programme for England. This means that farmers, as land managers, have to be increasingly well informed about their duties and obligations as well as their entitlement to various changing grant scheme payments.

But there have been some spectacular success stories. Most of Swaledale and Arkengarthdale was designated by the National Park Authority in 1989 as a Conservation Area. The National Park Authority was able to launch a Barns and Walls scheme in partnership with English Heritage, to give grants to help restore and repair barns at risk. By 2000, over 340 barns had been repaired and the scheme was extended into Littondale. The Yorkshire Dales Millennium Trust was also able to help restore another 60 barns outside the Conservation Areas. By 2010 it was estimated that almost 486 traditional farm buildings were restored and 87 maintained through these and other agri-environmental schemes.

It is calculated that between 1998 and 2010 something like 259km of drystone wall had been repaired or restored and 3,855km have been protected and maintained. Over a six year period between 1998 and 2004, grants of over £6.71 million were paid towards the repair of barns and walls in the Dales, totalling £9.34 million taking into account landowners' contributions. Most of this labour intensive work was carried out by local contractors. This is estimated to have contributed between £3.27 and £4.74 million into the local economy, producing what is known as an economic multiplier through the purchase of local supplies and services at a ratio of 1:65, a major boost for the Dales economy. This conservation work has also been an important creator of skilled local jobs, in such areas as stone wall building, masonry and carpentry, with small specialist companies emerging to fill the need, and even skill shortages, that YDMT have helped to fill by supporting apprenticeships and training courses in partnership with local Further Education Colleges.

But there are still many hundreds of barns and walls at risk outside these schemes, and maintenance is an on-going requirement. Ultimately there is little point in maintaining a building which has no practical use or economic function – though in some cases farmers have found that a newly restored barn is in fact often a useful building to have for storage and other purposes. Though many barns in village and farm complexes have been converted to residential use, perhaps to provide self-catering visitor accommodation, such as the very successful Bunk Barn project, or even for office or light industrial use,

Schoolchildren have been encouraged to investigate and record the number of plants flourishing in traditional meadows. Happily engrossed in their task as part of the Yorkshire Dales Millennium Trust's 'Into the Meadows' project are groups from Bainbridge Primary School and Settle Primary School.
(Tanya St Pierre – YDMT)

The Hay Time project has involved collecting Green Hay from herb-rich meadows so that its seeds can be used to improve species in other fields. Harvesting is here taking place near Bainbridge.
(Don Gamble – YDMT)

A different kind of machinery is used to collect Green Hay at Wharfe.
(Don Gamble – YDMT)

barns situated in the centre of outlying fields are not so easy to deal with. Conversion to housing may require unsightly new access roads, concrete parking areas, improved sometimes door sized windows, aerials, and all the suburban paraphernalia of modern living, which would dramatically change the nature of the very special landscapes. This is an on-going debate.

If walls and barns are important to the National Park, what about the hay meadows which are such a stunning feature of the higher Dales? The wonderful flower-rich meadows are at even more extreme risk. Incredibly over the last 50 years over 98 per cent of the UK's traditionally managed meadows have disappeared, replaced with bland, if productive, improved grassland of little botanic or wildlife value. Traditional meadows only survive in a few isolated pockets including, in England, the North Pennines and the Yorkshire Dales, which has precious flower-rich meadows in Upper Swaledale, Wensleydale, Upper Wharfedale, Littondale, Upper Ribblesdale and Upper Nidderdale.

Maintaining, and if possible increasing the number of traditional meadows in the Dales, is more than a question of nostalgia or aesthetics. There are good scientific reasons to maintain species-rich meadows, which can hold up to 120 different varieties of plants. These provide a vitally important genetic bank of species which could for future generations hold a key to much new scientific research, for example in drug therapy, medicines or agriculture. Many experts believe that climate change, with drier summers and perhaps harsher or wetter winters, will impact on vegetation and on agriculture, especially on more marginal hill land as in the Dales. It is likely that species rich meadows will actually prove more adaptable and more resilient than improved monoculture grassland, which is dependent on high regular doses of nitrogen-rich fertiliser to thrive, all of which has to be produced at high energy and transport cost.

Old meadows are also rich in insect life, including butterflies, bees, and in small vertebrates on which much other wildlife depends. Together with roadside and railway verges, ironically even motorway verges,

they form important corridors for wildlife which again with climate change may be vital for species survival, especially if, as many scientists predict, there will be species migration northwards as climatic conditions change.

And finally the ancient meadows of the Yorkshire Dales and North Pennines have a high potential value for sustainable tourism. Just as people flock to Japan at cherry blossom time, or to New England for the spectacular leaf fall, there is every reason to suggest that, done in an appropriate way, visitors could be invited to the Yorkshire Dales especially to experience the spectacular, colourful meadows in late May and most of June. With good public access, including in Swaledale stone paved paths through the meadows, and ample local accommodation, weekend flower breaks could be a very special kind of experience.

One of the Yorkshire Dales Millennium Trust's most imaginative and perhaps far–reaching schemes, developed in partnership with the Yorkshire Dales National Park Authority and supported by Natural England and the Yorkshire Wildlife Trust, as well as a host of other partners, has been what was known as the *Hay Time* project, and continues as the YDMTs popular *Flowers in the Dales* project.

Established in 2006 *Hay Time* had the initial aim of restoring at least 200 hectares of upland and meadow within and close to the National Park. Its prime aim is to *'work with farmers to restore meadows across the Dales'*. With a full time project officer, initially Pippa Rayner and later Christa Perry, the project became two sister projects in the North Pennines AONB and the Yorkshire Dales National Park. The priority was to give practical help and advice to farmers, many of them already in existing Stewardship schemes, of how to best manage and increase the biodiversity of their meadows. Key has been the collection and storage of flower seeds, including Green Hay, and to work with farmers to get the wildflower seeds planted in the right conditions for the new species to take hold. Green Hay is about cutting standing hay from an existing herb-rich donor meadow and scattering it on the prepared soil of the recipient meadow, to allow the new meadow quickly to absorb the seed and to help it germinate. Special machines were also devised, working with a local contractor, to gather and scatter seeds to allow wildflowers to spread.

Equally important to the practical work has been the awareness raising about the importance of meadows as a unique and very special part of the heritage of the Yorkshire Dales. This educational work has continued through the annual YDMT *Flowers of the Dales Festival* when from spring and right through the summer, a large number of events linked to looking at not just the meadows but a wide variety of Dales flora, has established itself as part of the Dales calendar. A book *Hay Time,* published by YDMT, with essays by various leading experts and edited by project manager Don Gamble, and former project officer Tanya St Pierre, remains the definitive guide to Dales meadows, their barns and walls, putting the story of the Dales meadows and their protection into context, highlighting the many places where flowering meadows can be experienced without compromising their quality.

But flowers are important not only in the meadows of the valley bottoms. English Nature – which in 2006 became Natural England – had long had concerns that upland limestone grasslands in central and western areas of the Dales were losing much of their biodiversity and variety through overgrazing by sheep, whose teeth, like little razors, soon cut grass and other vegetation on a Dales hillside to a smooth lawn. In 2002 a project was launched over 1,500 hectares of limestone upland on the slopes of Ingleborough, including the National Nature Reserve, Upper Malhamdale, Malham Moor and Upper Wharfedale. Known as *Limestone Country*, the project was undertaken in partnership with the National Park Authority, the National Trust (a major landowner in the area) and several other partners, and directly involving 17 Dales farms. As this was in a Special Conservation Area, it was part funded by the EU Life Fund.

The aim of the Limestone Country Project was to increase biodiversity by replacing sheep grazing by hill cattle, and in particular to introduce some of the older hardy beef breeds which were no longer in fashion such as Belted Galloways, Shorthorns, Blue Greys, Highland and Welsh Black. Some of these such as Blue Greys would have been a common sight in the Dales 60 years ago. The older breeds of cattle prefer to chew blue moor grass typically avoided by sheep and Continental cattle breeds, as well as other tougher, dominant grasses, thus allowing other plant species including native wild flowers to flourish. Cattle hooves also break up the soil, allowing wildflowers to seed and flourish.

The scheme has remained an outstanding success, even after it came to a close in 2008. Project Officer Louise Williams not only persuaded many farmers to take part in the scheme, but encouraged a new pride in the revival of the old beef breeds that they knew as children, when their fathers and grandfathers farmed. The high quality, lean beef they produced soon had a ready market in local butchers' shops and restaurants, and even the better supermarkets. It was realised that the provenance of beef from Dales limestone pastures made it a quality premium product, especially valued in the decades after the Mad Cow BSE tainted meat scare. The winning of an international *Eurosite Award* in 2005 for the project did much to establish Dales Limestone Country beef, like the famous Wensleydale cheese, as part of a real Dales experience.

Both the *Hay Time* and the *Limestone Country* Projects have built important bridges between those who live and work in the Dales, whose love and pride in their rich natural and cultural inheritance is made tangible by these projects, and their many thousands of visitors can now share this experience. In so doing traditional meadows and flower-rich limestone pastures make a valued contribution to the local economy. To understand and appreciate is also the first step in acting to cherish and protect, whether by making a donation to the Millennium Trust or other supporting charities, or ensuring that our elected politicians recognise that environmental protection is not a luxury to be slashed at a time of alleged economic difficulty, but essential for our long term physical, emotional and mental well-being, and even for our ultimate survival.

Chapter Five

Saving the Green Lanes

If you were to name the oldest man-made feature in the landscape of the Yorkshire Dales, it would have to be the ancient green lanes, sometimes surviving as a broad green swathe enclosed between drystone walls, sometimes a rough track cutting across open moorland, linking daleheads, often taking the most direct line through the hills and between valleys, the natural routes for a walker or rider. Incised into the hillside by generations of feet and hooves, the oldest green lanes date back to Bronze Age times or even earlier, ancient trade routes crossing the Pennines, taking advantage of natural passes between the hills, or along the high edge of a dale to avoid swamp, rivers and forest in the valley floor.

In later years some were developed into campaigning roads for the occupying Roman legions, for example Stake Pass between Wharfedale and Wensleydale built by soldier engineer Julius Agricola in the first century AD. In medieval times some became busy packhorse trails, linking outlying settlements with market towns. Most splendid of all perhaps are the magnificent wide drove roads, such

as Galloway Gate above Dentdale, used by drovers bringing their cattle down from Scotland to be fattened on the sweet pastures of Malham Moor, or Mastiles Lane, that celebrated drove road between the monastic granges of Malham and Kilnsey and their parent Abbey of Fountains.

Other roads were later used by wagons and even coaches, roads such as the Cam High Road between Ribblesdale and Wensleydale, part of the main route between the port of Lancaster and the North East, until replaced by the Lancaster-Richmond turnpike road in the 18th century. New turnpike roads built in the 18th and 19th centuries, with better surfaces and easier gradients suitable for faster stage and mail coach horses and eventually motor vehicles – generally our modern 'A' and 'B' roads in the Dales – left the older roads to the mercy of the Pennine weather. They finally crumbled to loose stone, soon covered by grass, those quiet "green" lanes only to be frequented by the occasional sheep and curlew – and in more recent times walker, cyclist or horse-rider.

It is a great principle of English highway law, dating back to the time of King Alfred, that 'once a highway, always a highway'. The right to walk, ride and even take a wheeled vehicle along these old roads, remains even if the public authority no longer recognise or maintains them, though now almost all are recorded on the Definitive Map.

In legal terms the name 'Green Lane' is meaningless. They are only 'lanes' in the sense of being highways – that is having a right of public passage, either only on foot, on foot and horseback or indeed by horse and cart – though the ancient law doesn't actually distinguish between a mechanically driven vehicle and a horse and trap.

Until recently, their legal status was a minefield,

Walkers and cyclists were long able to enjoy Mastiles Lane as a green sanctuary of timeless peace and beauty. This view from the 1950s shows two cyclists descending towards Kilnsey. (Alan Parker)

with the old tracks suffering from a bewildering range of legal definitions, some lost in time. Often recorded as Roads Used as Public Paths (RUPPs), it was often difficult to know exactly what public rights existed on them. The CROW Act 2000 sought to get rid of the confusion for once and for all, by requiring local authorities to record and classify all such unsurfaced RUPPs either as Byways Open to all Traffic (BOATS) or Restricted Byways which could only be used by walkers, horse-riders, cyclists and wheeled vehicles which were not mechanically propelled – i.e. horse drawn carts or carriages.

However this reclassification did not solve the problems of what are known as Unsurfaced, Unclassified County Roads (UUCRs), or sometimes White Roads as they are shown on the OS maps. What is often unclear is exactly what rights exist over them. This includes the curiously named 'ratio tenure' roads maintained by the landowner or tenant, not the highway authority, whilst others are purely private access tracks to a house or farm.

The whole controversy surrounding which of the old green lanes could be used by motorised vehicles – i.e. motor cycles and all terrain cars – has in part been driven by technical developments in vehicle design, and the subsequent growing popularity of off-road motor sport vehicles among newly affluent urban dwellers who see the rugged countryside of the Yorkshire Dales as the ideal setting for their activity.

Until the 1970s the number of off-road motor cyclists was relatively small. In the Yorkshire Dales it was very much a fringe activity, mainly led by the Trail Riders Fellowship – a national organisation with local branches that campaigned very effectively to safeguard the rights of mainly middle aged motor cyclists in the countryside, to ride old roads and tracks with vehicular rights.

There was also a parallel popular tradition in the Dales of motor cycle trials, including the famous annual Scott Trial in Swaledale, which originated as a mainly off-road endurance 'trial' of bikes and riders from Shipley in West Yorkshire as early as 1914. By the mid 1970s the number and frequency of such trials, which take place with the landowners'

permission in various parts of the Dales, had all been carefully regulated by both the National Park Authority and the police, with promoting groups working hard to minimise surface damage and to ensure all litter is removed. Trials might be a serious nuisance for anyone seeking peace and quiet on the day in question, but they avoid using public rights of way and generally take place on private land.

However, in 1986 a new organisation known as the Land Access and Recreation Association was formed, with strong support from the motor industry. Originally known as the Land Access and Rights Organisation, its name was soon changed to the less militant sounding present form and acronym LARA – a girl's name – carefully concealing the fact that they are actually an off-road motor using pressure group.

To a considerable extent the emergence of LARA reflects the growing popularity of more affordable, four-wheeled drive, all-terrain vehicles, not just the ubiquitous Land Rover, but new smaller imported vehicles, now available to a much larger percentage of the population. Once acquired, such a vehicle offered a chance to enjoy off-road driving as an exhilarating and challenging activity away from tarmac roads, even before the popular TV programme *Top Gear* was launched to glamorise the activity among adolescent boys of all ages.

LARA, even more than the TRF, had learned from their opponents in the Ramblers that they needed to prove that ancient vehicular rights of way existed over ancient green ways which might otherwise be classified as bridleways. Just as the Ramblers employed specialist and amateur lawyers to research old deeds, documents and Enclosure Awards and if necessary to take contested cases to court, LARA quickly drew up lists of routes throughout the UK where they believed there was strong evidence of vehicular rights.

Such lists were soon distributed across the fledgling internet and drivers were making their way to areas such as the Dales to explore the old trails. To be fair, LARA, aware of their image, also took care to educate their own members into a more responsible use of the countryside in terms of keeping just to routes where there was some evidence of legal right, driving safely and heeding the needs of others, and in later years to avoid sensitive places. They were also very adept at ensuring they were well represented on all official national and local countryside consultative bodies, including the new Access Forums, to ensure that off road drivers were regarded as legitimate and responsible users of the countryside, who had as much legal right to use the tracks as the walkers or horse riders.

LARA also ensured that when it came to the reclassification of RUPPs, whenever there was evidence of vehicle use, even of horses and carts over a century ago, such routes should be shown as BOATs and not a Restricted Byway.

Walkers, conservationists and many landowners didn't quite see it that way. It was fairly clear throughout the 1980s and 90s that something dreadful was happening to the green lanes of the Dales. Not just more trips in 4x4s by established groups such as the Pennine Land Rover Club, but by many more individuals in powerful luxury vehicles such as Range Rovers who saw huge motorised adventure sport opportunities in the Dales. But as a few moments looking at web sites will soon demonstrate, for the hard-core enthusiasts the real excitement of a day out off-roading is to try and get your vehicle in as difficult and challenging a situation as possible and use the power of the machine and skill of the driver to thrash heroically through.

In so doing, however, devastating damage can be done to the ancient highway in question – not just tyre marks and surface damage, but often huge ruts and mud, quickly impassable in wet weather. On open moorland this often results in tracks spreading up to five vehicle widths, a sea of mud reminiscent of the First World War. Getting a vehicle stuck in some deep crevice and organising a rescue complete with power winches is a thrilling highlight of some enthusiasts' day.

But the damage wasn't confined to track surfaces. On one particular stretch of Mastiles Lane, the local farmer Mr Carr of Lee Gate Farm, on Malham Moor, was incensed to discover that his wall tops were being used to put under the wheels of stranded 4 x4s to

haul them out of the ruts. Archaeology in the form of the foundations of the small Roman fort on Mastiles Lane was also being damaged.

Walkers and cyclists, who until then had been able to enjoy Mastiles Lane as a long green sanctuary of timeless peace and beauty, were horrified about the damage. It became almost impassable in places, somewhere to avoid especially at weekends when you could come face to face with threatening fleets of 4 x 4 drivers or leather clad motor cyclists roaring towards you or, even more alarming, behind you.

Many other moorland tracks were now claimed as having vehicular routes, such as the Horsehead Pass between Langstrothdale and Littondale, the Stake Pass to Semerwater, Gallowgate and the Occupation Road in Dentdale and the great and beautiful ancient Highway over Cotter End and Mallerstang between Wensleydale and the Eden Valley. Even quite remote mountain paths, such as the Walden Road over the shoulder of Buckden Pike into Starbotton were invaded by trail bikes, an alarming experience for walkers having literally to dash for safety as bikes roared and bounced over the shoulder ridge of Buckden Pike.

When public meetings were organised by parish councils or conservation groups in the Dales to discuss the growing problem, meetings were often filled with leather jacketed motor cyclists, easily intimidating local people in the meetings and preventing any open discussion or effective decisions being taken.

At first the National Park Authority were remarkably equivocal about the damage and conflicts, taking the view that as off–road users had rights of access, it was the Park's job to protect those rights as surely as they would for walkers or horse riders. On one occasion, faced with photographic evidence of deep ruts on Cam Road, it was even suggested the damage had been done by walkers.

The Yorkshire Dales Society and the Campaign for National Parks realised that something had to be done. The YDS, with support from the Ramblers, helped to establish the Yorkshire Dales Green Lanes Alliance. By bringing together walkers, conservationists, parish councils, farmers and

Mastiles Lane suffered devastation when it was increasingly seen as a challenge for off-road enthusiasts. This Range Rover has come to grief in 2002, despite stones being removed from a drystone wall to put under its wheels. (Mike Bartholomew – YDGLA)

The same location in April 2013 after a Traffic Regulation Order had prohibited use by recreational motor vehicles. This famous 'green lane' could at last be restored to its former glory. (Mike Bartholomew – YDGLA)

The first eight Traffic Regulation Orders included Cam High Road, which was suffering severe damage from off-road vehicles. (Author)

landowners, a truly effective group emerged. Under the expert guidance of chairman, Mike Bartholomew, YDGLA not only could match LARA in its understanding of the law, but were a highly effective lobbying group, working in partnership both with CNP and the National Green Lanes Environmental Action Movement (GLEAM), who are based in the south of England where similar problems, for example on the prehistoric Ridgeway, were just as acute.

What caused a major change in attitudes within the National Park Authority was an awareness of what is known as the Sandford Principle. Basically this reflected the recommendation of the National Parks Policy Review Committee, chaired by Lord Sandford, which reported in 1974. Its key recommendation was that if and when there is a conflict between conservation and recreation in a National Park, then conservation must take priority:

'National Park Authorities can do much to reconcile public enjoyment with the preservation of natural beauty by good planning and management and the main emphasis must continue to be on this approach wherever possible. But even so, there will be situations where the two purposes are irreconcilable...Where this happens, priority must be given to the conservation of natural beauty.'

This principle was one that ran through much of the Authority's planning and policy work, but what was happening in the 'Green Lanes' was its first real hard practical test in terms of a recreational activity in the Dales.

Faced with the graphic, well researched written and photographic evidence provided by YDGLA and supported by bodies such as the YDS, CPRE and local wildlife groups, it was clear that if the Park Authority was to uphold the fundamental Sandford principle, it had a duty to act.

The most powerful piece of legislation to protect green lanes, even where vehicular rights existed, was the Road Traffic Regulation Act 1984 which gives local highway authorities, that is County Councils, the power in a National Park or an AONB to close roads fully or partly, not only to protect the green lanes from damage, but (section 22) for the purpose of 'conserving or enhancing the natural beauty of the area, or affording better opportunities for the public to enjoy the amenities of the area, for recreation, or the study of nature'.

This wasn't just a question of preventing damage to surfaces, but reducing the intrusive noise of vehicles in the quiet heartland of the National Park, as well as the physical threat to other users of often fast moving vehicles on a narrow track. Tranquillity is, or should be, part of the experience of a National Park, to be able to hear the sounds of the natural world, not the scream of an internal combustion engine. Off-road vehicles not only damage the natural environment, they also totally destroy the pleasure and enjoyment of others. By 2000 the National Park were taking matters seriously, gathering evidence and consulting on key routes, and in 2003 were able to persuade the County Council to put Temporary Traffic Regulation Orders on four key routes, but only because of severe damage to the track surfaces caused by motor vehicles. But these restrictions applied only for a few months whilst repair work was done, and the Park had to constantly urge NYCC to extend the restrictions. It was not a satisfactory solution.

The problem lay in the fact that the highway authorities, in the case of the Dales, the Cumbria and North Yorkshire County Councils had little interest or appetite to do anything. It was suspected that highway engineers might have more sympathy with the motor lobby than the conservationists, and action seemed unlikely.

Then, in a superb example of how environmental networks can work, CNP, well briefed not only by GLEAM and YDGLA, and in partnership with the National Park Authority, was able to work closely with its members and colleagues in both Houses of Parliament, and with key civil servants, to get a vital

amendment in the Natural Environment Rural Communities Act 2006, at that time going through Parliament. Section 72 now gave National Park Authorities, not just Highway Authorities, the power to impose Traffic Regulation Orders on a byway or unsurfaced road for the same reasons as indicated in Section 22 of the 1984 Act. This was a huge breakthrough.

Taking on board sensitivity assessment principles first established in the North Pennines AONB, rather than going for an unworkable blanket ban, a clear framework was established to deal with green lanes in the Dales at risk. Unsealed routes were classified by the National Park into the most vulnerable routes at high risk of damage and disturbance to wild life as well as humans, areas at medium risk where use needed to be monitored, and areas of low risk where, because of hard surfaces and location, less problems were occurring. But often it is a question of scale of usage – one or two vehicles per day might not be a problem, but when it reaches the scale as was observed over Deadman's Hill between Coverdale and Nidderdale, used by over 100 bikes in one day, things are clearly getting out of hand. The celebrated and by now severely damaged Mastiles Lane became the first battleground.

But to ensure that all users had a say in the decision making process an informal consultative group, Yorkshire Dales Green Lanes Advisory Group, was set up, with representatives of motor vehicle users as well as walkers and cyclists, to try and achieve consensus wherever possible. This included encouraging responsible behaviour on routes where rights existed, and avoiding or reducing conflict between users. But where conflicts remained and environmental damage was occurring, action would be taken by the Authority.

In 2008 the first eight Traffic Regulation Orders were made, soon followed by five more. These included such iconic routes as Cam High Road, the Carlton to Middleham track, Foxup Road, Gorbeck Road, The Highway, Horsehead Pass, Ling Gill, Long Lane (Clapham - Selside), and of course Mastiles Lane.

But the battle was far from over. In 2009 LARA

challenged the eight Orders in both principle and detail in the High Court. But the National Park Authority stood its ground and all but one, Gorbeck, were finally confirmed. Part of Gorbeck Lane and its linking Stockdale Lane from Settle were however later determined to be bridleways and therefore finally protected from the severe damage which was then being inflicted by motor vehicles.

It was a momentous victory for the whole principles on which the National Park was based. This included setting aside at least some remote, traffic free areas where landscape and natural beauty can be enjoyed free of the physical threat and noise from motor vehicles, surely every bit a human right as the motor sport enthusiasts energetically claimed rights to enjoy their off-road activities in many other areas.

The National Park Ranger service (as it is now known) produce an annual report on 'green lanes' management in the Park and review how effective the Orders have been. Another major breakthrough has been the willingness of the North Yorkshire Police to give vigorous support to the National Park Authority in dealing with drivers found ignoring Traffic Regulation Orders, with threats to impound vehicles if offences reoccur.

If the saving of Mastiles Lane and the other routes at greatest risk was a great victory, another very different and much more positive development on the usage of the 'green lane' inheritance began when the National Park Authority, in partnership with Natural England, took on the task of completing the vision in the Dales of the late Lady Mary Townley. A keen horsewoman, in 1986 Mary rode from Derbyshire to Northumberland using available bridleways and unsurfaced tracks to highlight lack of provision for horse riders. She subsequently proposed a Pennine Bridleway, a new National Trail for horse riders, cyclists and walkers to complement the Pennine Way. The idea was supported and is now a reality. Of the 80km (52 miles) in the Yorkshire Dales National Park, several sections involve use of now protected ancient green lanes, including Long Lane at Clapham, Galloway Gate, and now forming part of the popular Settle Loop, Gorbeck Lane, the very same magnificent green lane over the open moorland between Ribblesdale and Malham Moor that had been rescued from trashing by the 4x4s and trail bikes by the National Park with a TRO.

But the constant threat from those whose idea of enjoyment is to create maximum noise and damage to the magnificent green lanes of the Yorkshire Dales remains. With cool aplomb the motor lobby have even set up an organisation known as the Green Lanes Alliance – a piece of identity theft designed to mislead. In a strange way it is also a tribute, a recognition that they have been countered by the stubborn commitment and professionalism of the Authority, supported by the excellent YDGLA with the wider support both of local communities within the Dales and the wider outdoor amenity movement. But constant vigilance, as ever, will be needed.

Protection of the 'green lanes' heritage of the Yorkshire Dales is therefore an example of the Sandford Principle in action, safeguarding something very special in the cultural landscape of the Yorkshire Dales for the present generation and for those yet to come.

Percival Brothers, a lively little company, provided bus services in Swaledale until 1971. The alternative of using a car did not seem to be widespread when this photograph was taken in Reeth in the 1950s. (Ron & Lucie Hinson)

The last through train on the complete length of the Wensleydale railway pauses at Garsdale station April 1954. There was a wreath on the front of the locomotive, but otherwise there was little fuss at a time when railways were increasingly seen as an anachronism.
(J W Armstrong Trust)

Chapter Six

The Green Travel Revolution

In April 1954, a few months before the designation of the Yorkshire Dales as a National Park, the last passenger train, hauled by a small tank engine, clanked its way along the single track Wensleydale railway between Northallerton, Leyburn and Hawes. The spur from the Settle Carlisle line between Garsdale and Hawes lingered on with a skeletal train service until March 1959. Until 1964 the line remained open purely for freight between Hawes and Northallerton, though it enjoyed a short period of revival in the long winter of 1963 when, with roads blocked by snowdrifts, it was the only way of getting milk out and essential supplies into the Dales.

In Wharfedale the line between Ilkley and Skipton, which even in the early 1960s carried packed Sunday and Bank Holiday trains from Leeds to Bolton Abbey, was an early victim of the Beeching Axe in 1965, though it was later to be restored between Embsay and Bolton Abbey as a heritage line, the Embsay Steam Railway. The direct line to Lancaster was cut from the Leeds-Morecambe line in 1965 and most intermediate stations on the Settle-Carlisle line were closed in 1970. Even the once busy Darlington-Richmond branch, despite serving the troops of Catterick Garrison, lost out to a ruthless second wave of post Beeching cuts in 1970.

For many people in the 1960s, railways were an anachronism, a transport mode of the Victorian past, outmoded, expensive, soon to be replaced with 'more efficient' road transport.

Buses for a time continued to flourish. In the Dales buses were mainly operated by the three near monopolistic regional companies, West Yorkshire Road Car Company of Harrogate to the south and east, United Automobile Company in the two northern dales (though a lively little company known

as Percival Brothers lingered on in Swaledale until 1971) and Preston-based Ribble to the west. However in Airedale and Ribblesdale another independent, Pennine Motors, operated from Skipton to Malham, Ingleton and Settle. In 1969 Ribble, West Yorkshire and United all became part of the massive National Bus network, with each company retaining its own identity until privatisation took place in 1988. Pennine Motors however, with its distinctive orange and brown buses, still survives, a rare example of a small family-owned bus company dating from before the Second World War.

In general, until the 1980s, rural bus services enjoyed a degree of cross subsidisation from their more lucrative urban routes. The bus companies made enough money on their busy interurban and urban routes to be able to support their less busy rural routes, arguing, sensibly, that these feeder routes also brought passengers onto their profitable urban networks, in the same way that railway branch lines which appear to lose money actually help make the trunk route profitable. Sadly successive politicians and their advisers, blissfully ignorant of the complexities of transport economics, argued the opposite, eventually even making cross subsidisation illegal. This was to have disastrous consequences, just as it had on the immediate post Beeching railway network, not only for people living along rural bus routes, but ultimately for the trunk routes themselves as they no longer received traffic to and from the unprofitable feeder routes.

Bus services prior to the mid 1980s were also highly regulated by the Traffic Commissioners set up in 1930 to prevent duplication, wasteful competition and sometimes even irresponsible and unsafe behaviour by some operators, and to ensure high standards of vehicle maintenance and safety. Head to head competition along the same routes was not permitted. Timetables and fares had to be approved by the Commission, and this helped to create a stable network, something that was to change in the late 1980s as a result of the 1985 'deregulating' Transport Act.

In fact though bus services were far more frequent in urban areas and along the main roads, in rural areas such as the Yorkshire Dales the picture was much more mixed. Some dales, now totally bereft of buses except for Sunday DalesBus services, such as Upper Nidderdale or Littondale, had better services. There were also popular market day services, for example from Skipton to Hawes every Tuesday and to Leyburn every Friday. Sunday and Bank Holiday services however were often quite sparse, the exception being West Yorkshire Road Car Company which realised from the early 1950s onwards that there was money to be made from well promoted weekend bus services from urban West Yorkshire into the Yorkshire Dales, with services between Leeds and Bradford to Buckden and Hawes aimed at walkers and more general visitors.

By the 1970s both West Yorkshire Road Car from Leeds, Bradford and Harrogate and United from Darlington were promoting their Sunday networks into the Dales as their Dales Rider and Dales Rover leisure networks, with their services into Upper Wharfedale, Malhamdale, Wensleydale and Swaledale. The classic was Service X72 running a Saturday and Sunday bus from Leeds to Bolton Abbey, Grassington and Kettlewell over the Kidstones Pass to Aysgarth Fall and Hawes. This Sunday and Bank Holiday bus still operates as the 800 Yorkshire Dalesman service as a core part of the summer Sunday DalesBus network.

But in truth, just as people had abandoned the trains for more convenient buses and cars, by the 1960s bus services were also losing patronage to the car. Whilst there had been less than a million cars on Britain's roads in 1949, by 1967, just 19 years later, this had shot up to 14 million. And it would soon race past the 20 million mark. In 1951 47% of people in Britain used trains to access their holiday destinations, with 27% travelling by bus and coach, identical to the 27% who travelled by car. But by 1968 66 % were taking their holidays by car, whilst bus and coach usage for holiday visits had declined to 16% and rail to only 14%.

It was a self-perpetuating circle of decline. Loss of passengers led to reductions in services and closure of railways, rapidly accelerating after the implementation of the Beeching Report of 1963. This led to further passenger losses as faced with a worsening service, or no service at all, passengers turned to their cars. Whilst rail closures might boost traffic on the buses for a time, most people found slower bus travel, soon subject to heavy traffic congestion, a reason to acquire a car. With rising personal incomes throughout the 1960s and 1970s, and improvements in car design and ever reducing costs in real terms, cars were now more affordable, with hire purchase deals and a good second hand market, for people on even average incomes. A car offered freedom and flexibility; with a car on the drive you were no longer the prisoner of the bus or train timetable, you could go where you wanted when you wanted. The car-owning democracy was born.

Mass car ownership also changed the nature of rural tourism. No longer confined to a number of train or bus accessible seaside or inland countryside resorts, with a car you could travel to and stay overnight in places well away from a railway station or even a bus stop. Driving through the Dales – 'touring' – in your own car with family, luggage, even pets, became a leisure activity in its own right. Visitors could now reach the remotest valleys and villages along a much improved road network. Guidebook writers could direct their visitors to the wildest locations, to park their cars to climb hills and fells formerly well outside the range of a normal day visit. The first instructions in most walking guidebooks were now where to park your car not to where to get off the train or bus.

This boosted Dales tourism as many small hotels and guesthouses well away from a bus or train route could now receive visitors, even low season or on days such as Sundays when in many areas many buses

A return Easter excursion train leaves Grassington for Bradford in the early 1950s. Although this branch line had closed to regular traffic over twenty years earlier, it was still popular with Bank Holiday crowds. (David Joy collection)

did not run. On the other hand some of the traditional inland resorts such as Ingleton, once a visitor hot spot which lost its railway station in the 1950s, and which was in later years to have a much reduced bus service, soon began to lose its peak weekend crowds. This also meant the visitors came more sporadically, at less fixed times compared for example with the Bank Holiday crowds that even until the 1960s poured off special excursion trains at places like Bolton Abbey, or Threshfield for Grassington, where the little branch line from Skipton, closed in the 1930s, stayed open for freight and summer excursion trains.

But the new leisure traffic also brought new problems. Surveys by the former West Riding County Council Planning Department indicated that on one typical fine summer Sunday in July 1967, 22,000 vehicles entered the National Park carrying 50,000 people. Over 3,000 cars were recorded that

day on the Bolton Abbey B6160 road and 2,000 on the B6265 Skipton - Grassington road. It was estimated that on that same evening only a couple of hundred people were staying in the nine Youth Hostels that at that time were open in the Dales. The traditional hiker with khaki shorts and hob nailed boots, or cycle tourist with his Sturmey Archer gears, saddlebag and thick tyres, staying in a Youth Hostel which at that time didn't permit motorists to stay, was in sad decline.

It was calculated that with planned new motorways and planned road improvements in the 1960s and '70s, there would soon be five million people within an hour's drive of the Yorkshire Dales National Park and 16 million within two hours.

National Park planners believed that it would soon be impossible to cater for all these visitors and their cars without massive new car parks and huge road improvements, including road-widening schemes

Challenge Walks have become immensely popular – and especially so in the Three Peaks where their management has become a major issue. There can be serious problems with over-use of paths, although this is unlikely to have been a cause for concern when one such walk was photographed in Kingsdale back in the early 1960s. (D M Petyt)

that would dramatically alter the character of the area. Large new car parks did indeed soon begin to appear at various 'honeypot' locations such as Clapham, Grassington, Aysgarth Falls, Hawes, Malham, Stainforth and even Dent. Visitor facilities such as Information Centres were increasingly focused around the car park, and information services offering circular self-guided walks focused on the new car borne visitors.

Fears of massive road improvements that would change the character of the National Park to accommodate the new generation of motorised visitors lay behind a concerted campaign during the 1970s by the Campaign for the Protection of Rural England to save the Dales from what was identified as 'death by a thousand cuts' – an on-going programme of road improvements, removing bends and straightening roads, widening sections to allow traffic to move faster, removing hazards to safety but at a price of demolishing old walls and even buildings. It was rightly believed that part of the appeal of the Dales is its characteristic winding, stone-walled lanes – even main roads – which are landscape features in their own right. Smooth straight carriageways built for faster cars and in particular for growing numbers of heavy quarry wagons, for example on the B6265 between Swinden Quarry and Skipton, or the B6479 between Settle and Horton in Ribblesdale could dramatically urbanise a landscape which had taken centuries to evolve. It was felt that this must not happen to all roads in the National Park. There needed to be a strategy to ensure that whilst some major roads had to be improved, the rich heritage of minor lanes and tracks should remain as they were, part of the landscape heritage.

In 1978 CPRE published a booklet *Motor Traffic in the Yorkshire Dales* which suggested which roads in the Dales should be protected. This was to form the basis for what became the farreaching *Advisory Road Hierarchy for the Yorkshire Dales* published in 1981 by the Yorkshire Dales National Park Committee in partnership with North Yorkshire and Cumbria County Councils. This divided up the roads in the Dales into six categories, according to the actual

The success of the highly innovative Dales Rail venture in 1975 spearheaded the reopening of several closed stations on the legendary Settle to Carlisle railway. Among them was Dent, miles from the village it purports to serve but magnificent in its remoteness. (Graham Lindley – YPN)

traffic function of the roads. Category I Primary distributors for through traffic were mainly motorways and trunk roads outside the Park. Category II Secondary Distributors used for main delivery vehicles and coach traffic would only be improved with great care to manage the landscape impact, Category III Tertiary Distributors, such as the main roads in Upper Wharfedale and Swaledale, had an important traffic function but would not to be improved except on the most urgent safety grounds, with all but essential local and visitor traffic being discouraged. Categories IV and V were Local Roads and Access Roads, the very special and vulnerable winding Dales lanes which apart from essential resurfacing would remain unchanged. The lowest category VI – unsurfaced tracks and green lanes – has been dealt with in Chapter 5. But it is worth recalling

that as late as the early 1970s there was an attempt by the Skipton Area Surveyor to tarmac Mastiles Lane, a threat that became a national issue with letters in *The Times* and petitions of several thousand signatures.

This Advisory Document, which was adopted by all the authorities, has served the Park well. It offers guidance to planners, who in theory can deter large scale leisure or development from taking place on unsuitable roads, and also to highway engineers who can at one and the same time focus their activities, including road signing, on the most important roads in terms of their function, keeping the precious heritage of old walls and winding lanes of the Dales protected by mutual agreement. There is little doubt that it played a key role, when in the 1980s there was a concerted attempt by highway engineers to improve and sign the A684 as a Trans-Pennine Heavy Goods Vehicle route between the M6 in the west and Teesside, to help justify a major new bypass around Hawes. This would have had a devastating landscape impact, generating huge extra traffic through other villages, and the Advisory Road Hierarchy was a valued tool in arguing against the scheme. Opposition was supported by the then Richmond Member of Parliament, Leon Brittan, and the project was quietly, and hopefully permanently, shelved.

CPRE and others have also attempted with some success to extend this concept to the protection of roadside verges. These are marvellous havens for wildflower and other plant and insect life, a rich reservoir of biodiversity. Cutting the verges too early in the year destroys both flowers and seed, as does parking on the verges. The Yorkshire Dales Millennium Trust, the Park Authority and Nidderdale AONB have worked with highway authorities on verge management schemes to ensure that this very precious living part of the landscape heritage of the Yorkshire Dales is also protected.

In fact despite the alarmist forecasts of the traffic planners, the numbers of cars did not increase exponentially through the '80s and '90s as the survey graphs seemed to predict. If anything during the last two decades traffic pressures seem to have levelled off. Traffic jams still occur on fine Sundays on access roads to Bolton Abbey, and honeypots like Malham or Ribblehead still have huge lines of parked cars on the approach roads to the village or near the cross roads on fine weekends, but these are the exception. Perhaps, as some surveys have suggested, with early retirement and more shift working, mid-week visits are now more popular. Better outdoor clothing encourages people to spread their visits to the shoulder months and even in winter rather than cramming them into the few short peak weeks of summer, to avoid the very traffic jams that in the 1970s seemed to occur much more frequently. Maybe with Sunday leisure shopping and huge retail parks on the motorways for some people retail therapy has become a substitute for a drive through the Dales. Other leisure attractions, including theme parks, fun runs, mountain biking in some of the

Forest Parks now offer greater attraction to a family than perhaps a walk around Ingleton Falls or Hardraw.

An exception perhaps has been the Three Peaks Walk – the 25 mile 5,000 feet challenge circuit around Penyghent, Whernside and Ingleborough, which has become such a draw for not only those who want to prove something about their physical fitness and endurance but also for organisers of Challenge Walk fund raising schemes. The huge popularity of the Three Peaks Walk – not just the cycle cross event but the major charity walks – can result in up to 1,000 pairs of feet tramping the route on a busy Saturday. Most participants despite the nearby railway come by car. Part of the National Park's excellent Three Peaks Project has been both to raise funds to restore and protect the footpaths, encouraging walkers to avoid vulnerable areas, and to find ways of managing parking and traffic in the village.

One imaginative and perhaps visionary solution to the problems of visitor traffic was developed in the 1970s – and that was Dales Rail. In 1975 the then Yorkshire Dales National Park Committee started the germ of what can now be considered a green transport revolution by chartering a series of special trains from the cities of Leeds and Bradford in urban West Yorkshire along what was the already threatened Settle-Carlisle line. The pilot scheme had the train running over three weekends in May, June and July 1975, calling at what were then four closed stations in the National Park – Horton in Ribblesdale, Ribblehead, Dent and Garsdale plus Kirkby Stephen before continuing to Appleby where the train was stabled, but the Saturday service continued to Carlisle for shoppers as well as being a walkers' train to Carlisle, with a second train in the reverse direction operating for shoppers into Leeds.

The success of the Dales Rail service to some extent revived the Ramblers special trains of the 1960s. Crowded trains had to be strengthened and the pilot scheme extended over the rest of that summer. In 1976 – stations on the Eden Valley at Langwathby, Lazonby & Kirkoswald and Armathwaite were also opened.

Dales Rail was not however just a train service. Buses were planned to meet trains at Garsdale from and to Hawes and Sedbergh, extending over to Swaledale and Barbondale, on Saturdays also bringing in local people for shopping trips to Leeds or Carlisle. In addition a programme of guided walks from the train and buses were provided using experienced walk leaders, initially from the Ramblers Association.

What was therefore being offered was not just a train trip, but a whole day out in the grandest and most majestic scenery of the National Park. It was an educational experience – delivering a greater understanding of the National Park as well as a greener way of reaching and experiencing the Park.

The cost of a day out was deliberately kept to little more than the equivalent cost of petrol – the perceived marginal cost of using a car – so that even for a couple it was actually cheaper if parking charges, wear and tear and other hidden overheads were included. Bus travel was integrated with train tickets so that you could book a through ticket to Hawes or Sedbergh. Both British Rail and the bus companies cooperated fully.

It was a Swiss or German style integrated travel experience, but with the added element of the involvement of a National Park in its promotion and interpretation. Dales Rail was a major success story. Within a couple of years it led to a separate Lancashire Dales Rail service being provided, originally from Manchester and Blackpool over the freight only Blackburn-Hellifield line. The Lancashire Dales Rail still continues. The reopening of Clitheroe station, like the other stations initially only on an 'occasional' basis, was the first stepping stone in the full reopening of the Ribble Valley line from Blackburn to Clitheroe and current aspirations are to reopen to Hellifield on a daily basis.

Dales Rail was also a pioneer on the Wensleydale railway in 1979 and 1980 with an occasional Dales Rail Wensleydale service from York or Newcastle, again fed by connecting buses to and from Swaledale and Upper Wensleydale at Redmire station. But funding cuts and problems caused by a freak blizzard in late April led to this Dales Rail service along the Redmire line being abandoned until revived by the Wensleydale Railway Company in 2003. The line is now operated by WRC at weekends and holiday times between Leeming Bar and Redmire with vintage diesel railcars and occasional steam trains, and the whole line may soon be reopened between Northallerton and Redmire on at least a seasonal basis.

Dales Rail soon built up a large body of regular users of the Settle – Carlisle line. When closure of the whole line was announced in 1985, these leisure users proved critically important in helping to save it, joining forces with local authorities and more traditional rail enthusiasts to help sway public opinion. But Dales Rail also demonstrated the huge economic importance of the railway in bringing visitors into the Dales, not just passing through, but alighting from local stations and connecting buses to spend time and money in the area.

Even more exciting developments were to follow when in 1985 the local stations were audaciously reopened on a daily basis, initially to get college students to Carlisle at a lower cost than bus transport. With the initiative of Settle-Carlisle line manager Ron Cotton, who ironically had been appointed to oversee the closure of the line, the summer weekend Dales Rail now became a fully restored, all-year local train service. Not only were the Dales Rail walkers a core market for the new service, but groups such as the Friends of the Settle Carlisle Line and the Friends of Dales Rail volunteers took over from the National Park as champions of the line, helping to promote and publicise the route to their own membership and a wider public, leading guided walks and planning a variety of events to bring new people to the line. This is a role which was also taken forward by the Settle Carlisle Enterprise Network (SCENE) and the Settle-Carlisle Development Company, creating a blueprint; developing a model of community and business involvement in a local railway, which has now become one of the major visitor attractions of the North of England, as well as a key transport artery and local rail service in its own right.

But the National Park Authority didn't just focus

Another reopened Settle – Carlisle station was Ribblehead, seen here against a backdrop of snow-covered Whernside. (Author)

A diesel unit at Redmire station, the terminus of services operated by the Wensleydale Railway Company. (Author)

on train services. It was realised that the bus network – now branded as DalesBus in a subtle tribute to Dales Rail – served many areas of the National Park and indeed neighbouring Nidderdale AONB to access places trains could never reach. Increased car ownership by the 1980s made even the popular Sunday leisure services uneconomic and services were soon under threat. Provided they were subject to a competitive tendering process, local authorities could now offer what was known as revenue support to help maintain them. Without such public sector support most of the rural bus routes in the Yorkshire Dales would have disappeared by the 1990s.

The National Park Authority through its Transport and Visitor Management Officer Andy Ryland worked with the County Council to secure funding for a network of Sunday buses, with additional revenue support and marketing help from the National Park's own budget. But the threatened cuts to the Sunday DalesBus network, most especially the popular service 803 between Leeds and Swaledale, had resulted in the setting up, in 1996, of the Yorkshire Dales Public Transport Users Group which changed its name, in 2012, to the more succinct Friends of DalesBus.

One of the first actions of the new Group was to organise guided walks off the DalesBus network, replicating the success of Dales Rail and the Friends of the Settle Carlisle line in helping to fill the buses even on winter Sundays. The Group also worked closely with the National Park Authority on the very successful EU-funded TARGET project launched in 2002, designed to develop and promote sustainable transport. Excellent new publicity did much to boost the ridership of DalesBus, and one of the most innovative projects was the provision of a cycle-carrying bus, using a 24 cycle carrying trailer, which operated between Wakefield, Ilkley, Grassington and Kettlewell. Another was the simple but effective DalesBus green logo, now carried on all the popular Sunday DalesBus services.

Whilst there was delight in 2006 when the Yorkshire Dales Target project won the coveted Ecologically Sound Travel Award offered by the Austrian Government, this delight turned to despair

The new face of bus transport in the Dales. (Author – 3)

The Sunday Cravenlink Dalesbus service collects a passenger outside Strid Woods, Wharfedale.

Service 808 from Hawes arriving at Ribblehead station in time to meet the train from Leeds.

The Yorkshire Dalesman – one of the popular Sunday Dalesbus services – picks up a passenger at Bainbridge on its way back from Hawes to Leeds and York. (Paul Kirby)

A pioneering service conveying cycles in a trailer operated on summer Sundays from 2001 until 2005. Sponsored by the National Park, it ran between Wakefield, Leeds, Grassington and Kettlewell.

when it was realised that the massive cuts to both the National Park and North Yorkshire transport budget would put the award winning network at risk in 2007. How could this meet the criteria of sustainability?

In addition came the news that in July 2006 North Yorkshire County Council and West Yorkshire Integrated Transport Authority – Metro – could not agree to the funding of the cross boundary Sunday X84 bus service between Ilkley and Skipton – a key link into onward service to Malham, Grassington and the Settle - Carlisle railway. The operators First Leeds had no option but to withdraw the service.

Faced with the loss of these key links, the Yorkshire Dales Society and the YDPTUG, who had already funded a series of special monthly 803 service to help fill what they saw as a gap, took a brave and radical step. It was to set up a form of social enterprise, one of the earliest Community Interest Companies in the north of England. It was agreed to establish the body – technically an asset locked company – within the Yorkshire Dales Society, a charity, to give it the security of a parent body, an office address and both volunteer and professional support. It was named the Dales & Bowland Community Interest Company to reflect what seemed to be a possible role to help to save the also threatened Bowland Transit Bus network within the Forest of Bowland AONB.

Established in 2007, the first success for the CIC came when the Yorkshire Dales Society was able to secure a Yorkshire Dales Sustainable Development Fund grant of £20,000 for a project known as *Sharing the Dales*. This was used not only to restore the Ilkley-Skipton Sunday bus service, not directly along the A65 between Ilkley and Skipton, but branded as Cravenlink, also serving the National Park going via Bolton Abbey, Strid Woods and the village of Embsay. In addition a new monthly bus service to Malham, which had lost its regular Sunday bus service, was targeted through the Mosaic Project to ethnic minorities as well as to other less affluent young people and families. The project worked with individuals and groups especially from Huddersfield and Bradford, providing a programme of guided walks to get people out into the National Park using the new Cravenlink and Malham buses.

The success of the project, not only meeting but beating both passenger and financial targets, enabled the D&BCIC gradually to expand the network of services. Now came some new funding directly from the National Park, Natural England and even the County Council to compensate for cuts elsewhere. But when this new funding too was cut a couple of years later, the CIC had to seek new sources of support. The most important of these was West Yorkshire Integrated Transport Authority – Metro – which because of the value of DalesBus to West Yorkshire people, agreed not only to sponsor several of the key services out of urban West Yorkshire – Leeds, Bradford, Otley, Ilkley and Dewsbury – but to offer holders of the weekly, monthly and annual Metrocard commuter tickets free travel on the network. This made Leeds one of the few city regions in Europe where your weekly travel ticket to work could also be used in a National Park at the weekend. Vital too was the marketing support provided by Metro, including the popular DalesBus pocket timetable booklet, which contained details of all bus services in the Dales, an invaluable Dales green travel guide.

But an even worse blow was to come. In 2011 North Yorkshire County Council announced they were to withdraw funding from all Sunday bus services in the county, not just the limited support they were giving the CIC for DalesBus. This put two more vital routes in the Dales under immediate threat, routes equally important for local communities as they were for visitors. With its limited resources the CIC had therefore to rescue the key Skipton-Grassington 66A service in Wharfedale and Northallerton-Leyburn-Hawes 156/157 services through Wensleydale. Things looked desperate.

When in the autumn of 2011 the Government announced a new source of funding for rural buses, the Local Sustainable Transport Fund, the D&BCIC and Friends of DalesBus were successful in getting approximately £45,000 per annum from this Fund to support the developing DalesBus network over the next three years out of a total allocation of LSTF

Cycling in the Dales was still a relatively rare event when this photo was taken in the early 1960s. Proper winters were then a regular occurrence, but these three hardy souls are undeterred as they head down towards Burnsall from the heights of Greenhow Hill. (Bertram Unné)

funding of £1.1 million for the Dales areas as a whole.

By 2013 the DalesBus had grown to a network of twelve integrated bus services from towns and cities such as Leeds, York, Bradford, Wakefield, Dewsbury, Harrogate, Darlington, Lancaster, Burnley and even Manchester, all of which integrated fully with local train services, with excellent local publicity, in print and on the web, plus a range of interavailable rover tickets, and a programme of guided walks. Numbers of passengers have grown to total approximately 48,000 annual passenger journeys on the Sunday and Bank Holiday DalesBus network, an approximately threefold increase in the number of people travelling compared with those using the network in 2006. Despite this success, at the time of writing in 2014,

there is no certainty of future funding, and the D&BCIC is having to continue to stress the important economic, social and environmental value of DalesBus to the Yorkshire Dales National Park in meeting many partner objectives in the hope that sufficient funding can be secured for future years.

But funding has been less of a problem for that other important green travel revolution – cycling. For more than four decades the story was one of steady decline as heavy visitor and local traffic forced traditional cyclists off the crowded, polluted and dangerous roads. But in the 1990s came two crucial developments.

First was the national network of waymarked quiet lane and off-road cycling routes, secured and developed through the decade and into the next

Cycling has now caught the popular imagination with thousands taking to the minor roads and lanes around the National Park. This rider is enjoying glorious conditions as he heads past Penyghent towards Halton Gill. (Welcome to Yorkshire)

century as part of the National Cycle Network by the cycle route building charity Sustrans. Several of these routes such as Route 68 through the Dales, the 170 mile Roses Way Link between Morecambe and Bridlington through the heart of the National Park, or the more longer established 130 mile circular Yorkshire Dales Cycle Way using minor roads and lanes around the National Park, have caught popular imagination and brought literally thousands of people back to the joys and benefits of longer distance touring cycling.

The other key development is the astonishing growth in interest and activity in mountain biking, exploiting the network of 'green lanes', byways and bridleways through the Dales. This new wave of cycling activity is typified by the success of the Dales Bike Centre in Fremington, near Reeth, Swaledale which combines mountain and hybrid bike hire with the promotion to novice and experienced cyclists alike of a choice of spectacular off road routes across the moorland edges and former mining areas of the Dale.

In 2014 these trends have come together with the starting of the Tour de France – Le Grand Départ

Cycling in the Dales took a new dimension when it was announced that the 2014 Tour de France would pass through the heart of the National Park. Its route included a long climb from Wensleydale over to Swaledale, here being faced by a group of three cyclists. (Welcome to Yorkshire)

from Leeds and York, and going through the heart of the Dales. This will put the Yorkshire Dales as a magnificent destination on the European tourism destination map, and also give a huge boost to the joys and benefits of cycling as a recreational activity. With the creation of more quiet-road and off-road routes away from heavy traffic –and the new Pennine Bridleway is an outstanding example – the Yorkshire Dales is once again becoming as important a destination for cycling as it is for walking. Cycling is once again a mainstream activity, one that is bringing much younger generations of more active visitors back into enjoying and experiencing the National Park in a car-free way.

Even though the total number of green travellers, as a percentage of the eight million day visitors, over 90% of whom come by car, is still small, the Yorkshire Dales is increasingly recognised as a nationally important area to experience sustainable forms of tourism, at the heart of which are greener forms of travel.

Long may the Green Transport Revolution in the Dales continue.

Virtually every village in the Dales
once had its own water-powered mill.
Beamsley mill was originally built for
corn grinding and later became a
sawmill. (N R Thompson)

Chapter Seven

Green Energy – Threat or promise?

If you walk on Grassington Moor above Yarnbury, continuing above the great smelt mill chimney beyond Hebden Gill, if you look carefully in the rough grass and reeds you will detect a network of overgrown channels, usually filled with water, running down the moor. These are the remnant of what was once a highly sophisticated system of over six miles of narrow aqueducts, coming down from Priest's Tarn, and fed by becks from the nearby peaty summit of Meugher.

The water, gathered in a series of catchment ponds, regulated by small weirs and dams, once powered a series of waterwheels, connecting rods and ropes which in the last years of the 18th and the early 19th century helped to drain and provide power for the great Grassington Moor lead mines and ore crushing mills. At this time not just Upper Wharfedale, but Upper Nidderdale, Swaledale and Wensleydale were all highly industrialised areas. Lack of alternative fuel led to the Cornish and Derbyshire engineers hired by the Duke of Devonshire and other landowners to use water power technology, originally developed by German engineers from the Harz and Erzgebirge mountains. As coal was difficult and expensive to transport – though there were some poor quality mines high up on Barden Moor – water power was a highly cost effective solution. But after the mines closed from the 1880s onwards, water power ceased to have any importance.

It was a similar situation with the network of water-powered corn and textile fulling mills, which from medieval times onwards were to be found throughout the Dales, harnessing the power of local streams through a series of mill ponds damming the streams with goyts to channel water to the great wheels which could be up to 36 feet (11 metres) in diameter.

Improved communications, most notably the Leeds - Liverpool Canal and the Richmond, Wensleydale and Settle-Carlisle railways, soon allowed high quality coal from Yorkshire pits to be brought quickly and cheaply even to the Yorkshire Dales, with coal-powered steam engines soon driving the few larger cotton and wool mills in the Dales able to withstand competition from industrial Lancashire and West Riding. In the 20th century oil brought in tankers by road and rail took over. Petrol and then diesel engines replaced horses and steam, and like most rural areas of Britain the Yorkshire Dales eventually became almost totally dependent on the petrol or diesel car, van, lorry and tractor, with abundant electricity available through the National Grid, created from seemingly unlimited supplies of distant fossil fuel driven power stations to power domestic and industrial appliances.

Even as recently as the early years of the National Park, the last few working farm cart horses were still being replaced by more efficient tractors, steam locomotives were still to be heard panting their way over the Settle-Carlisle line and steamrollers were repairing Dales roads. There were even still a few farms not yet served by electricity depending on oil lamps and coal boilers.

Cheap energy has helped to shape the world we now live in, and is especially true of the Yorkshire Dales. Dales communities are heavily dependent on very high levels of car ownership and usage, with most households having access to two or more cars. Farms could not exist without the high degree of mechanisation they now enjoy. Homes are usually now heated either by oil, or in the larger

New perceptions of energy
conservation are bringing
significant changes to the buildings
of the Dales. These solar panels are
on a barn roof at Broadshawe, on the
Chatsworth Estate at Barden Fell.
(Dorian Speakman)

Grassington Moor with the smelt mill
chimney on the horizon. The whole of
this area has a network of overgrown
channels once forming part of a
sophisticated water-supply system.
(Robert White – YDNPA)

communities, natural gas.

The climatologist and TV presenter Paul Hudson has pointed out that in terms of energy consumption, rural communities in North Yorkshire consume far more energy per household than their equivalents in cities like Leeds or Bradford, with higher fuel consumption to heat larger, less well insulated homes, compared with a small city terrace or apartment, and relatively long car journeys to work or to access shops, a doctor's surgery or leisure centre, which in cities may be accessible on foot or by regular bus service.

But in the closing decades of the 20th century, our perceptions of energy have changed radically. First is the awareness of the impacts of climate change and rising CO_2 which as most independent experts throughout the world agree is not only now happening but is largely driven by the unrestricted burning of fossil fuel. Secondly, it is also apparent that with world population growth and the expansion of industrialisation into Asia and eventually Africa, demand for oil and even coal will outstrip demand.

The search for alternative fuel sources has intensified, especially for the so called renewables such as wind, solar and various forms of bio-fuels produced by growing trees or green matter which can also be converted in the relevant anaerobic digesters to produce gas to provide heat.

Fluctuating fuel costs provide a huge threat to the Dales economy, not only impacting on local people's mobility, but also on the number of visitors who come to the area with their spending power. With around 90% of visitors arriving by private car, higher fuel costs mean less spending in the local economy, especially in communities which are further from the larger centres of population such as the northern dales – Swaledale, Wensleydale and Dentdale. This in itself is a powerful argument to retain and develop high quality public transport networks for visitors and local communities alike.

Government targets, reflecting EU legislation, are set out in the UK Renewables Obligation which by 2020 requires electricity supply companies to source 15% of their energy from renewable sources – wind, water, solar, biofuels. This has in turn led to a major investment programme in wind power, with a heavy investment programme by both UK and mainland European companies seeking to take advantage of generous tax concessions and subsidies of around £400 million per annum (in 2012) for a crash programme to build as many wind turbines as possible.

No issue has divided communities and individuals more than wind turbines. To many people, especially environmental green groups such as Friends of the Earth, they are constructions of elegance and beauty, symbols of a responsible attitude to saving the planet. To others, including many walkers and National Park campaigners, they are an abomination, industrial scale intrusions in otherwise unspoiled landscapes, with a similar visual impact to great lines of pylons carrying the National Grid as well as more localised local transmission cables. Many campaigners point ruefully to the success stories in areas such as the Lake District and the Yorkshire Dales of undergrounding of transmission systems to remove the clutter of masts and cables across some of the finest areas of landscape, only to now face structures up to 120 metres high on the skyline.

Both sides are polarised with arguments about the efficiency or otherwise of turbines, their weather-dependent intermittent reduction requiring back up system in periods of still weather, plus their impact on bird life, for example as at Killington, above Lunesdale, where a major scheme as well as being visually intrusive could affect bird life on a nearby lake nature reserve. But others point to the huge reduction in carbon emissions, and suggest that as this is the greatest challenge for the future of the earth and of humanity, such considerations should overrule any subjective views about landscape quality.

Policy decisions by Government have however indicated a veto on the largest turbines in National Parks and Areas of Outstanding Natural Beauty, but smaller, more localised wind energy schemes can form part of climate change adaptation and mitigation strategies which, following a key DEFRA 2010 Circular, now have to be adopted by National Park Authorities in their Local Plans.

However the veto on large turbines does not apply outside National Parks, and battle lines have been drawn between landscape lovers and environmentalists supported by energy companies around the edges of National Parks. The concern in all the National Parks is that restriction, though welcome, will result in a "ring of steel" in terms of the erection of scores of the latest generation of super turbines around Park boundaries, so that the view from any fell top is dominated by slowly turning blades on every horizon.

The five turbines erected in 2006 at Lambrigg Fell west of the Howgills encapsulate the arguments. These medium sized turbines are visible from many of the surrounding fells as well as from the main A684 between Kendal and Sedbergh. They generate enough power for 4,000 homes and save 14,000 tonnes of carbon per year, with a life of 25 years after which the site can in theory be returned to its original state. But can these gains offset their visual impact? As always opinions are polarised between those who see them as a desecration and those as a piece of modern sculpture enhancing a dreary moor, which as some people would argue has been denuded of natural forest by mankind for the purposes of fuel gathering and sheep grazing.

Wherever a major scheme is launched, local action groups spring up which in turn are derided by the pro-turbine campaigners as NIMBY groups. But in the Yorkshire Dales, the National Park Authority has also taken a leading role in objecting to schemes which will be visually intrusive for key places within the National Park, for example on the skyline such as at Whinash in Cumbria, in the hugely attractive fell country between the western boundary of the Yorkshire Dales and eastern boundary of the Lake District National Park along the M6 Lune gorge corridor. This scheme was turned down at a Public Inquiry. A further victory was at Chelker Reservoir, between Bolton Abbey and the A65, where four small turbines that had been there for 20 years were to be replaced by two 75 metres giants. When it was clear that strong objections would remain, the application was withdrawn. However a similar scheme at Brightenber on the Craven drumlins, near Gargrave,

has experienced repeated applications by German based EnergieKontour for three 100 metres high turbines, which will be visible for many miles, including from many high places within the Park.

Given the intense level of controversy over almost all land based schemes, developers and government are increasingly looking for sea based off-shore solutions, but issues remain such as threats to bird life, increased costs and shore based transmission cables to serve the new installations.

But what of other, perhaps less contentious ways of dealing both with climate change and the new energy crisis? Far from being negative, the Yorkshire Dales National Park Authority has issued (2011) a comprehensive *Guide to Energy Production in the National Park* which sets out ways not only to help builders and developers meet green energy requirements in planning terms, but offer positive ideas, suggestions, advice and examples of good practice.

Fundamentally, solutions need to focus on small-scale local projects which do not inflict massive impact on the environment, but also reduce transmissions costs and energy loss in that transmission. There is a stress on energy conservation and insulation measures as a fundamental first step. Saving energy is the top priority. After that there are a variety of solutions such as small-scale turbines, which on a farm or in a larger settlement can fit in with existing buildings. Solar power is another solution, again siting panels on south facing slopes for efficiency, but at a scale which does not dominate the landscape. Wood fuelled heating systems are also supported especially when this can be linked to nearby woodland management.

Another major way forward is using Ground Source Heat Pumps which have a long life after initial capital costs, as have Water and Air Source Pumps. Several examples of highly successful schemes are quoted such as the Bike Centre at Fremington that uses Ground Source Pumps, or various domestic buildings and farms using solar panels, hydro and even small wind turbines. In terms of practicing what it preaches, the National Park's new Bainbridge

Wind turbines are either seen as desecration or modern sculpture. Yet there was certainly widespread celebration when the turbines at Chelker Reservoir were removed. They had long been conspicuous on the horizon south-west of Bolton Abbey. (Author)

Opposite: The changing scene on the River Wharfe at Linton.
Top: The weir photographed when the mill was still in use. (David Joy)
Bottom: Rising energy prices have now led to the river being used to power a new generating plant. (Author)

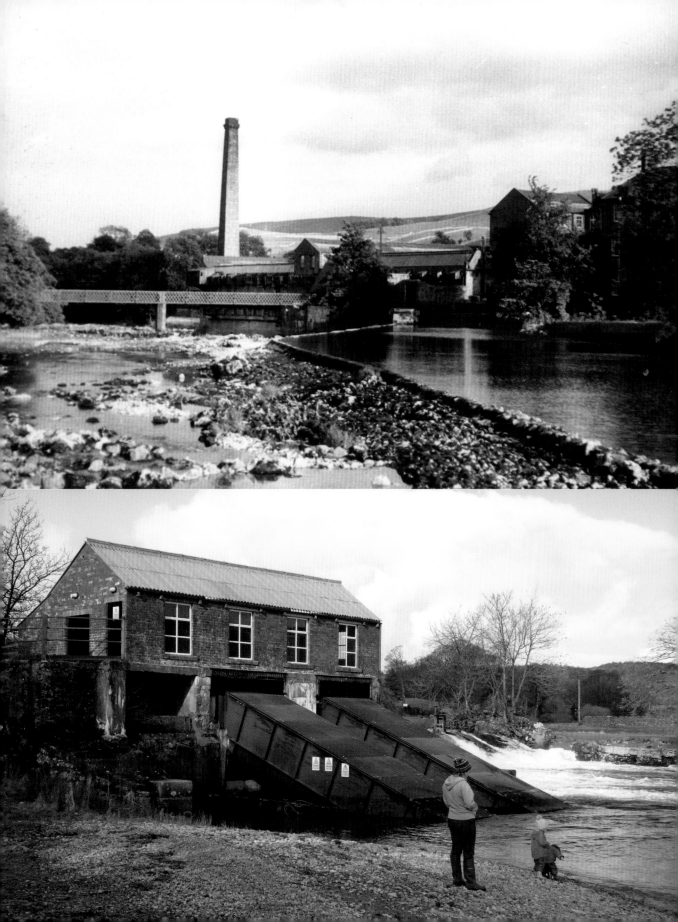

headquarters is virtually carbon neutral thanks to effective insulation and Ground Source Heat Pumps. One major gain in domestic or farm energy generation is that it reduces the need for unsightly transmission cables – a major gain.

Given the heavy rainfall in the Dales, and the large number of moorland streams and fast flowing rivers, hydro power is another key source of energy generation, reviving a centuries old source of renewable power and, compared with large wind turbines, offering little visual impact. The Settle Hydro was set up by a local group as an Industrial and Provident Society who raised the money with local shares and attracted grants to build the Archimedean screw generator on the Ribble, capable of generating 165,000kwh per annum, thereby saving 3,200 tonnes of carbon. Income is earned by selling electricity to the National Grid – the first hydro scheme of its kind in the UK to do so.

A similar scheme on the River Bain at Bainbridge – England's shortest river – uses another Archimedes-screw generator. The River Bain Hydro Ltd is also a Provident Society with a mixture of shares and this time a Charity Bank loan, with a target of 185,000kwh annually. But rising energy prices are now making this a commercial proposition for keen eyed investors, and the Linton Falls Hydroelectric Company is a commercial enterprise built by property developers JN Bentley. The generator, which occupies a historic Edwardian pioneering brick turbine house on the top weir on the Wharfe at Linton, near Grassington, is now producing 100kw or up to 500,000kwh annually.

But smaller schemes have a key role to play. One of the most imaginative is at Halton Gill in Littondale where what is known as a 'high head' micro hydro, developing 44kw, enough for twenty to twenty-five homes, brings a fast flow of water to a small turbine house, carefully designed by Langcliffe Hall Estate in partnership with the National Park Authority to look like a small farm outhouse.

The National Trust with extensive estates at Upper Wharfedale and Malham in the Dales has also shown the way with a number of small scale renewable energy schemes such as a small well sited wind turbine at Middle House on Malham Moor, providing many of the requirements for the farm. At Tenant Gill a combination of solar panels and a small hydro scheme meet the requirements of the farm. Batteries are used to even out peak and low peak power needs, with a backup generator in times of wind, sun or water shortage – which is rare. There are similar micro solar, hydro and wind generating projects at many other locations in the Dales, again actively supported and encouraged by the National Park Authority.

Solar energy, despite the fact that the Dales are cloudy and cool for most of the year, is still an important potential source of green energy – even weak sunshine can translate to significant heat and power. Even in conservation areas in the National Park, solar panels can be used if sited in ways which do not harm the visual appearance of buildings. In reality there is huge scope for solar panels in many farm complexes, for example on modern milking sheds and out buildings as part of the working farm. Equally valuable could be greater use of photovoltaic cells, now being developed in Germany and elsewhere, where roof tiles, for example looking exactly like ordinary slate or even stone, can generate energy from sunlight.

There are also moves in the Dales to develop anaerobic digesters. These need to be carefully sited, on farms and even for entire villages, in order to use organic waste and slurry which is converted by the action of bacteria into methane gas. This in turn can fire generators to produce electricity. The concept of larger Dales communities, with encouragement from the National Park Authority, developing into energy self-sufficient 'Transition Towns' is a very real one.

In this respect the National Park is providing exactly the kind of 'Greenprint' for a more sustainable future that Malcolm McEwan and others forecast should be the role of National Parks and other protected landscapes such as Areas of Outstanding Natural Beauty, making a long term contribution to both the future of the planet and to the national economy.

But the scramble for demanding new sources of

energy, renewable or otherwise, may also be a threat. It is unlikely that the geology of the Dales will ever make it suitable for hydraulic fracturing or 'fracking' – using massive water pressure to source huge reserves of shale gas. Nor are there opencast or deep mine coal reserves – the small coalfield at Ingleton was worked out some years ago. But biofuels could be a cause of concern if the scale grew to something beyond the merely local. The unsightly monoculture coniferous plantations of the 1960s and 1970s were until recently unharvestable because of the low value of the timber being produced, but new demand for wood fuel pellets has produced the first mass felling or harvesting of spruce trees since the 1960s, with the building of controversial new forest roads and access tracks, including the conversion of the ancient Cam Fell High Road between Langstrothdale and Ribblesdale for this purpose.

Could the Dales be seen as a place to grow new cash crops of willow, alder or poplar to convert to energy at distant power stations? Or even fast growing Switchgrass which could be seen as a 'renewable' solution to insatiable energy problems?

As Anthony Bradley argues in Chapter 8, Dales farmers have always had to adapt to external pressures and changing financial circumstances. If forms of support change for traditional Dales farming – whether sheep, beef or dairy – or if UK Government and EU support systems for looking after wildlife habitats, special landscapes and their visitors are reduced or even withdrawn, then we could see a loss of the great cultural landscapes and access to them that we so value, as various monoculture bio-fuel crops are planted even where soils are poor and gradients steep.

The omens are not good. At time of writing, the Government's liberalisation of the energy market and attempt to promote a decarbonisation of energy production could lead to a relaxation of planning regulations both for more transmission lines in protected landscapes, and incentives for biofuel production. Nuclear power, despite its huge costs and self-evident dangers, is back on the agenda.

There is an alternative solution to the dash for energy. It comes from putting conservation of energy at the top of the agenda, with insulating of existing and new homes an absolute priority, as this is where so much energy is wasted. Ironically the Dales produces huge quantities of one of the finest insulation materials known to mankind – sheep wool, which can be used to insulate both people and their offices and homes. Developments of the Passive House zero-carbon concept in the Dales may be increasingly relevant on both cost and environmental grounds. The second urgent requirement is transport, with a need to change the almost total car dependency culture of the Dales. Current national and local Government cost saving measures are cutting public transport provision in the Dales to little more than residual levels. This will make local people and visitors even more dependent on high energy consuming private cars and taxis.

Yet the development of so many interesting examples of self-sufficient renewable energy solutions in the Dales, linked to new individual and community lifestyle choices, might point the way for all of us towards a genuinely sustainable alternative to the high energy-consuming lifestyles that most of us are locked into. As costs and availability of energy become ever more problematic, and global warming impacts more evident, such radical ideas could become the only way for many rural communities to survive.

In a rapidly changing world, what is happening today in the Yorkshire Dales in terms of renewable energy could indeed be Greenprints for the future.

On the farms, the horse age was still giving way to the motoring age when the National Park was designated in 1954. The transition was not always without its problems, as seen here in Hebden Gill. Cattle, horse and rider patiently wait while the farmer tries to coax his vehicle into life. (YPN)

Chapter Eight

Farming in a National Park

Anthony Bradley

Despite my children thinking I am ancient, I was born after the National Park was established in 1954 so can't remember the early days of the Park. Though I do remember my father recounting how in 1960, when my mother was pregnant with me, our farm said goodbye to our last working horse, though by that time he was no longer a working horse. That in a way bookends the time and the farming traditions in the Dales that were ending just as the National Park was being set up.

Nevertheless there are still two things that characterise a Dales farm. Firstly the growing of grass because the land and weather preclude the growing of anything else. The western edge of the Pennines and their altitude catches lots of rain from Atlantic weather systems which in our case amounts to nearly 60 inches (152 centimetres) a year. We can have a first frost in September and a last one in May – as in the old saying of Dales weather being eight months of winter and four months of bad weather. Soils are often poor and incapable of taking a plough so the growing of commercial arable crops is a nonstarter.

A typical haymaking scene from the last days of the working horse. The unmistakeable peak of Ingleborough is in the background. (G H Hesketh)

Granddad could recall being asked to grow oats during the Second World War. Grow them he could, but ripen them he could not.

Secondly the only domesticated animals that can utilise grass are ruminants. The digestive systems of cattle and sheep get round the inability of standard mammals to digest the fibre and cellulose which are found in grass. Basically they have a large fermenting chamber – the rumen full of bacteria, protozoa and fungi that deals with the fibre and cellulose for the animal. It is then filtered and passes to a digestive system just like other mammals. Everything about agriculture in the Dales flows from the combination of those two basic processes of geography and rumination. Despite those constants, farming in and during the 60 years of the Dales National Park has changed largely because of forces well beyond local control.

In the 1960s it was possible to look out from our farm and count two dozen or so family dairy farms. If you listened carefully on Christmas Day the only thing you could hear was the faint buzz of milking machines. Those family dairy farms were supported by the interventionist mechanisms of the Milk Marketing Board. The MMB was set up in the 1930s to stop market abuse by the milk buyers – such as Granddad sending milk on the train to a dealer in Bradford, only for it to be returned the same day unpaid for. The MMB set the price throughout the supply chain, acted as a buyer of first and last resort and above all provided certainty. Farmers knew their milk would be collected and it would be paid for, on time, at a price they knew in advance.

The cows had changed from Shorthorns to Friesians and would be tied by the neck in shippons – the local name for a barn. They could spend up to eight months inside during the winter with the dominant forage being hay. These cattle would also receive cereal based feed – 'cake' – and often sugar beet nuts. These all came in paper sacks of half a hundred weight for the cake and an awkward sized hundred weight for the sugar beet. The cattle were all fed by hand and mucked out with a shovel and wheelbarrow. The same applied to the next two generations of growing heifers often housed in stone outbarns. Lots of manual labour, wild flower meadows and a couple of little tractors. We were typical in milking 40 to 50 cattle with 250 sheep, mostly Dalesbred, producing fat lambs and providing a living for three families.

The sixties and seventies were still a time when farmers were being encouraged to increase yields. Even more so when the UK joined the then European Common Market. Farm and herd size were increasing, assisted with grants to put up new buildings and technical advice from the Agricultural Development and Advisory Service (ADAS). This led the inexorable march away from hay making to producing silage as the winter forage of choice. The advantage of silage was more than the increased forage quality, reduction in weather dependence, mechanisation and increase in output per man, welcome though they all were.

But the big gain were the huge increases in grass yield. Nitrogen fertilizers used at ADAS recommended rates could increase grass output by as much as fourfold. Feed that to cattle with greater genetic potential, thanks to the use of artificial insemination, to produce more milk than ever before from that feed and there was scarcely a farmer anywhere who was not attracted to that. One man could milk, feed and muck out all in one building, two or three times the amount of cows giving twice as much milk than before this revolution took place. It did however mean goodbye to wild flower hay meadows. It also meant the amount of capital required went up, and an increase in farmers working on their own with the attendant financial and psychological risks rising as well. It was perhaps the high water mark for dairying in the Dales.

The 1980s brought the whirlwind of monetarism, laissez faire economics and Thatcherism. Butter Mountains and milk lakes proved that the post-war headlong pursuit of yield had worked. Post-war rationing was long forgotten and a public increasingly disconnected from agriculture demanded that the brakes be slammed on, much to the delight of the free marketeers dominating political and economic decision making in the Council of Europe. Welcome, in the early 1980s, to the world of milk quotas! These were especially tough on those farms that had spent money on expansion with a budgeted increase in milk production to pay for it. Capped production rather spoilt the sums to say the least. Quotas were tradeable –- either to buy or rent, but of course this added to production costs. What is more if you produced over your quota allocation, there was a fine to pay. Inevitably some dairy farmers decided enough was enough and quit milking cows.

The exodus from dairying was given added impetus in 1994 by the abolition of the MMB and when its successor Milk Marque – a voluntary co-operative – fell foul of competition laws. Many found that no amount of technical improvements could offset the deadly combination of quotas and a falling price for their milk. In the early 2000s that same view from our home could now count the dairy farms in Ribblesdale on the fingers of one hand. Dairy cows left the Dales and became concentrated in areas such as Cheshire and the South West. These places all had a more benign climate and geography, so could more easily cut costs of production. Given that the power of the grocery oligarchs grips ever tighter, one is bound to wonder if one day it will be necessary to reincarnate the Milk Marketing Board.

The Dales has a tradition, stretching back centuries, of raising cattle for beef as well as dairy. It had traditionally been an activity for more marginal farms in the hills as those in the valleys would milk albeit with dual-purpose cattle. The 1950s saw those traditional dual purpose breeds fall in popularity as dairy farms took up the higher yielding Friesians. The hills would support a variety of breeds that were crossed to suit a particular market. We had neighbours who had Blue Greys which were a cross between a Shorthorn and a Galloway. These had the milkiness of the Shorthorn and the hardiness of the Galloway. The Blue Grey would in turn have been crossed with a larger breed such as a Hereford or Angus to produce calves reared for meat. These terminal sire breeds were also being superseded by breeds such as Charollais, Limousin, Belgian Blue and Simmental imported from the continent. In turn the suckler cow became the continental cross from the dairy herd. In effect a modern dual-purpose cow.

These continental cattle produced large fast growing lean animals that were very adept at converting both grass and cheap cereals into meat. This was a big change from keeping native type cattle that had been bred for generations to produce meat from poor grasses in all weathers on the top of a hill.

The fifties and sixties also had guaranteed prices for beef with so called deficiency payments to make up the difference between the market returns and the target price. Following entry to the Common Market, the keepers of suckler cows were in receipt of the Suckler Cow Premium, all of which enabled farmers and their cattle to stay in business on those hills. So as dairying declined, many farms changed their cattle from dairy to beef. Some of the heifers produced would be reared as replacement suckler cows but many would be finished on cereals. The bull calves would no longer be castrated as in the past with slow growing native breeds. They could be reared to slaughter in a year or so, to greater weights and leaner carcasses. In effect farmers increased the yield of beef per acre not just with growing more grass but with cheap cereals and entire bulls.

But the stability in the beef industry was about to be overturned because in the background and quietly at first there was a new cattle disease emerging. It was soon to turn into a major food safety scare that rocked cattle farming to its core. Bovine Spongiform Encephalopathy (BSE) was acknowledged as a new disease by the government in 1987. With just a trickle of cases to start with and mostly in dairy herds, it flew, for a while, under the radar. Once cattle could no longer enter the food chain if over 30 months of age, spinal cords had to be removed from carcasses and selling beef on the bone was banned, it became more serious. By 1996 when the EU banned the export of beef from the UK, BSE was an existential crisis for beef farmers. The UK effectively became over-supplied and the laws of supply and demand dropped prices at a stroke. It was to be ten years before beef from the UK could be sold abroad again. In the meanwhile another crisis hit.

In 2001 came the carnage of Foot and Mouth, and the Dales was one of the hardest hit areas of the UK. In many ways it need not have been so bad for

A pair of Masham lambs pose for the camera before William Bradley feeds them. (Anthony Bradley)

A Swaledale tup at Ribblehead sheep fair in 1997. (Jim Moran – YPN)

A superbly evocative photograph of sheep above West Stonesdale in deep midwinter. It is bitterly cold in this hamlet at the head of Swaledale, although the farmer wears no gloves. (Bruce Greer – YPN)

farming or indeed the rest of the Dales economy. The lessons of the 1967 outbreak had been long forgotten: namely that as soon as FMD is first suspected, all animal movements in the whole country should stop immediately. (It was remembered in 2007 to good effect.) The government waited 5 days by which time the disease was out of control. It is then a deadly game of catch up which took the rest of the year. When restocking did eventually take place, numbers did not return to pre FMD levels – something incidentally that also affected those dairy farms still struggling on – as many farmers took the opportunity to reduce borrowings, or numbers, or retire. With the prospect in 2003 of the Suckler Cow Premium being abolished as the CAP reforms introduced the Single Farm Payment, hill farmers could collect their 'brown envelope' without keeping the numbers of cattle they had in the past. Cumulatively the effects of BSE, FMD and CAP reform – also ending the era of cheap cereals - has reduced the population of beef cattle in the Dales as much as, if not more than, the rest of the country.

In many ways sheep fit the particular natural challenges of the Dales best of all, but are also a natural foil on grass farms to cattle. Usually both are needed as cattle are not selective grazers and sheep will graze in the winter without damaging the ground. Just like cattle, the sheep industry has changed but perhaps in a more nuanced way. We still have a stratified sheep system with the horned breeds – now dominated by the Swaledale – on the highest ground producing their own replacements and crossed with a Blue Faced Leicester to produce Mules for breeding fat lambs on the better grazing lower down. The technical advances in grass growing means that some of those Mules now stay on their place of birth.

The tups the Mules run with to produce fat lambs have changed from mostly Suffolks to mostly Texels as they are much preferred by the supermarkets. Texels have also become a producer of breeding sheep as well as being the dominant terminal sire. Those farms with high fells and valley bottoms will have all the combinations. Every farm will choose to keep the breeds, crosses or combinations depending on their own situation. All these farms are reliant on the rest of the system. The fat lamb producer needs the Mules from the hills, but the Mule breeder needs the fat lamb producer to buy them. Unlike the cattle industry, sheep are not dominated quite so heavily by one or two breeds and despite the ubiquity of the Texel and Mule, there continues to be the traditional use of hybrid vigour.

So as first dairy and then beef cattle have left the best pastures and meadows, they have been replaced by fattening lambs. Local auction markets are still selling a similar number of lambs as in the past but now the balance has switched from store lambs – for someone else to fatten – to fat lambs. Some land that once produced milk and then beef now produces fat lamb. The technical advances in growing grass, making silage and large buildings are also put to use lambing sheep indoors. The prolific Mule needs to be well fed to carry and rear twin Texel lambs and for there to be sufficient grass in the spring pastures.

The sheep industry has also gone from guaranteed prices and rows at auction marts, with the Ministry grader checking that lambs had the correct fatness, to headage payments on ewes and then to Single Farm Payment. Top that up with huge losses on the back of FMD and sheep numbers are perhaps a third less than they were at the turn of the century. But the sheep industry has a different supply and demand situation from beef and dairy. Imported lamb from New Zealand is being increasingly directed to the emerging economies of the Far East. The UK also sends about a third of all lambs it produces to Continental Europe – and hilariously mostly to the French. Reduced home production, reduced imports and increased exports mean the UK grocery giants do not have it all their own way. Consequently the last few years have seen better prices for farmers – that is until the weather or our Irish friends occasionally spoil things. But it was ever thus.

The first 60 years of the Park look and felt tumultuous for farming, but in ways unrelated to the establishment of the National Park as such. The geography of the Park means pastoral farming. That farming produces the magnificent landscape that led to the original designation. We have always had short-term difficulties with severe weather, and there is nothing more soul destroying than digging out dead sheep and lambs from snow drifts. But that landscape and the way it is shaped by farmers has changed because of forces beyond and bigger than the National Park. UK and EU Agricultural Policy seemed too often deliberately to operate counter to the objectives of the Park and sometimes counter to the wishes of farmers, such as abolition of the Milk Marketing Board.

The 1990s and the introduction of the first Environmental Schemes was the beginning of a time when agricultural policy and National Park objectives became more aligned. The removal of headage payments following the introduction of the Single Farm Payment and later Entry and Higher Level Stewardship schemes added a further impetus to that change. However they do represent a huge cultural change for farmers. Farming has always been about producing as much food and to as high a quality as possible, given the natural constraints farmers operate within. Government support actively encouraged that until nearly the turn of the present century. Price and quality demands of the grocery sector now make that timeless ambition a necessity in order to survive economically. But the aims of Stewardship schemes and perhaps of the National Park are at odds with that business imperative. In some ways farmers are now being asked to face both ways.

Some farms have been able to take advantage of other opportunities associated with operating in the National Park. The last two or three decades has seen an inexorable rise in farm diversification. Indeed some of the Common Agricultural Policy budget has financially supported this rural development. From bed and breakfast provision for visitors to bunk barns, holiday cottages and camp sites, they have all taken advantage of on-farm assets and visitor demand. In effect farmers must now also farm – or at least look after –people. Farmers' Markets, food festivals, foodie culture and the internet have also helped some farmers escape the tyranny of the supermarkets. This mosaic of developments often starts as discretionary add-ons to the main farming business, but these activities are increasingly essential to family farm survival. But all such visitor-friendly developments stand on the shoulders of pastoral farming – our core business.

There is an irony that as direct support for agriculture has been withdrawn, food production in the Dales is now often being cross-subsidised by farming families from their non-farming income.

The magnificent gritstone crags of Mallerstang Edge tower over Little Ing Farm in the valley bottom. (Kyle Blue)

The Nab forms the characteristic jagged summit of Wild Boar Fell, from where Scotland can be seen on a clear day. (Kyle Blue)

The Northern Howgills contain some of the most spectacular scenery of the Yorkshire Dales and yet do not have any formal landscape protection. They are seen here at their finest on an early spring morning looking towards The Calf from a point between Langdale Knott and West Fell. (Kyle Blue)

Chapter Nine

Unfinished Business

One of the most thrilling moments in the northbound rail journey along the celebrated Settle-Carlisle line is when, north of Garsdale, the train crosses over the Aisgill summit and starts its long descent into the Eden Valley through Mallerstang, a valley of wild grandeur, with the great characteristic jagged point of Wild Boar Fell on your left and the magnificent gritstone crags of Mallerstang Edge to your right, glorious in later afternoon light.

Tom Stephenson, creator of the Pennine Way and one of the founding fathers of the National Park movement, once confessed that Wild Boar Fell was his favourite hill walk, a spectacular ridge from where you can see Scotland, the hills of Dumfriesshire across the Solway Firth.

Further west lie the Howgill Fells, those mysterious and lonely dome-like hills, celebrated by, among others, Alfred Wainwright, who described their appearance from a distance being like "velvet curtains in sunlight". He confessed that their "greatest appeal must be to those who love to walk freely 'over the tops' and commune with nature in solitude".

It is astonishing to realise that these wonderful areas, which contain some of the most spectacular

scenery of the Yorkshire Dales, do not have any formal landscape protection. Even the Howgills, which tower over the little town of Sedbergh – since 1974 transferred from the old West Riding of Yorkshire into Cumbria – are only partly in the National Park as far as the summit ridge of The Calf, up to a long forgotten county boundary with old Westmorland which ran along the ridge, a division that denies all logic of landscape quality or geography.

These great landscape areas, and much other fine countryside between the Lake District and Yorkshire Dales National Park, were excluded purely for political reasons and for administrative convenience.

The Friends of the Lake District, who as well as being guardians of the National Park also act as the Campaign for the Protection of Rural England in Cumbria, have long been aware of this absurdity, and from the 1950s onwards have campaigned to get these areas protected. In 1972 FLD submitted a paper to the Sandford Committee requesting that these areas be protected. In 1975 the Friends requested the Countryside Commission that the narrow valley above the Lune known as Borrowdale, plus Mallerstang and the Northern Howgills, should be considered for special protection.

In 1984 the Commission finally agreed to review the two National Parks' boundaries. Progress continued to be slow and half-hearted and was finally abandoned in 1992 on grounds of costs and lack of staff time. However, in 1987 FLD managed to secure the inclusion of Mallerstang into the Pennine Dales Environmentally Sensitive Area, which offered some support for farmers to help meet conservation objectives.

By the late 1990s it was recognised that these areas would be at increasing risk from such developments as wind turbines, new reservoirs and transmission lines, so in 2001, with the support of the Yorkshire Dales Society, FLD launched a Boundary Review Project to research what needed to be done to put matters right. A Key Supporters Group, consisting of officers and members of Friends of the Lake District, the Yorkshire Dales Society, Campaign for National Parks, plus a number of independent experts such as Lord Judd, Lord Clark, Sir John Johnson, Sir Martin Holgate, John Dunning, and former Countryside Agency landscape designation expert Ray Woolmore, was established to oversee the project.

It soon became clear to the Boundary Review Project Officer, Frank Lee, a retired Lake District planner, that at least as far as the Howgill Fells and Mallerstang were concerned, this was 'unfinished business' for the Countryside Commission, as successor authority to the old National Parks Commission, to complete. Both the Dower report of 1945 and the Hobhouse Report of 1947 had identified the Howgills as an area that met the landscape criteria for a National Park. Sir John Hobhouse, chairman of the Committee that bore his name, had suggested that special measures of protection should apply to certain fine areas of the countryside which he called Conservation Areas – and which were later to become the basis of Areas of Outstanding Natural Beauty. The Howgill Fells Conservation Area was one such area, which though it was deemed to be of sufficient quality to be in a National Park, was supposedly overshadowed by countryside of even higher quality – presumably the central Lakeland fells and the Ingleborough area.

When the North Pennines AONB was set up in 1988, it was agreed by the Commission to exclude Mallerstang and the Howgills from the AONB on the grounds that they should be examined in a future boundary review of the Yorkshire Dales National Park for inclusion within the Park, also including Middleton, Barbon and Leck Fell areas. The Commission went on to state publicly in 1998 that it indeed had 'unfinished business' in this part of the Pennines, and a duty to designate landscape which met the criteria for National Parks as set out in the 1949 National Parks Act.

Alun Michael, the then Minister for Rural Affairs, confirmed to the Countryside Agency (as the Countryside Commission then became) that it could change boundaries of a National Park without the whole boundary being subject to a review, a major time consuming process that would doubtless result in attempts to exclude as well as include areas currently within the Park in question.

This chimed in perfectly with the FLD's Boundary Review Project, and in 2005 the Project's report *Cumbria's Forgotten Landscapes* was published. The report sets out eleven key tests for the new areas to be included in the National Park – these were a) landscape quality – the most important consideration, b) landscape character, c) recreational experience, d) settlements which contribute to the special quality of the areas, e) an easily distinguishable physical boundary, f) sensible Local Government boundaries where they also follow such realities, g) avoiding cutting communities in two by boundaries through the middle of villages or towns, h) unsightly existing development to be excluded, i) areas where new quarrying and mining development may take place which normally would be excluded, j) features of scientific, historic or archaeological value, k) areas where easily identifiable transition between landscapes of different character is clearly visible.

This set out very clearly the shared vision of FLD and YDS for the extended National Parks, with detailed maps in the report outlining just where the new boundaries should run. For the Dales the proposed western boundary would take in the Middleton and Barbon Fells as far as the main road up the Lune Valley, to the north the Howgills as far as Tebay, and both Wild Boar Fell and Mallerstang north to Ravenstonedale and Kirkby Stephen, and east to join the existing National Park boundary east of High Seat above Mallerstang Edge. *Forgotten Landscapes* also perfectly reflected the Yorkshire Dales Society's own long held vision of these spectacular landscapes forming an essential part of the National Park.

The report also looked at an area of little known but beautiful limestone country to the north of the A685 Tebay-Kirkby Stephen road, known as the Orton Fells, which it was recommended should form a separate Area of Outstanding Natural Beauty. This area of around 200 square kilometres of predominantly limestone country includes ten Sites of Special Scientific Interest, fine areas of limestone pavement, two National Nature Reserves, two internationally recognised Conservation Sites and

131 listed buildings. It also has a number of areas of land open to public access under CROW legislation, an excellent public footpath network, and a choice of quiet lanes and bridleways for horse-riding and cycling. Wainwright's popular Coast to Coast Path also crosses the area between Shap and Kirkby Stephen, and has already brought tens of thousands of walkers into the area.

The Countryside Agency took this carefully researched report extremely seriously, and commissioned their own consultant, Alison Farmer Associates, to provide an independent assessment of the findings and the areas under investigation. Their report published in 2006 examined and even expanded most of the FLD/YDS recommendations but also concluded the Orton Fells were of sufficient quality to meet the criteria for National Park designation. Interestingly, among key benefits identified by the report was the integrated management skills that a National Park administration could bring to the selected areas within the landscape character areas as a whole, but also the continuity of funding that would be enjoyed rather than the ad hoc piecemeal nature of other schemes and projects outside a National Park management structure.

In 2006, Natural England, created from an amalgamation of the Countryside Agency, English Nature and part of the Rural Development Commission, took over the CC's role for landscape designations. Among their highest priorities, following the successful establishment of the New Forest National Park (which was delayed because of a High Court challenge) and the South Downs National Park, was what was now known as the *Lakes to Dales Landscape Designation Project*.

By 2009, serious progress on the project began with a lengthy programme of public consultations, meetings and discussions, and in the light of these consultations, further modifications to boundaries were proposed. In September 2011 a final decision was made by the Natural England Board to go ahead with the Boundary designation.

Differences between what was now proposed and the original FLD/YDS proposals were relatively

minor, and generally agreed, but one major difference was the decision to include the Orton Fells area within the Yorkshire Dales National Park, rather than establishing a free-standing Area of Outstanding Natural Beauty or even putting it into the Lake District National Park.

The reasons for including the Orton Fells in the Dales rather than the Lake District National Park were interesting. It was partially because the new area would be contiguous with the Dales, immediately across the A685, but more tellingly it was because the extensive areas of limestone pavement had greater affinity with the landscape character of the great areas of karst limestone scenery around Malham or the along the shoulders

Previous pages:

Top left: The little known Orton Fells have some fine limestone pavement, as seen in the foreground of this view looking from Muddy Gill Plain towards the Northern Howgills. (Simon Warner – Natural England)

Bottom left: Smardale Bridge on Wainwright's popular Coast to Coast Path is crossed annually by some 8,000 walkers. It lies on the section between Shap and Kirkby Stephen. (Kyle Blue)

Top right: The Lune Valley with the Southern Howgills in the background. Although nearby Sedbergh was included in the National Park in 1954, this wonderful stretch of river fell outside its borders. (Simon Warner – Natural England)

Bottom right: The extensions in the 2012 National Park Order include the northern tip of Lancashire close to Kirkby Lonsdale. On the edge of this town is the famous Ruskin's View. (Simon Warner – Natural England)

of the Three Peaks.

Support for the new landscape designation, despite the hostility of a small minority, was overwhelming, with over 68% of those consulted in favour, an over two to one majority. Support was strong from among local communities in the new areas to be designated as well as from visitors. Farmers generally welcomed the potential extra support for agri-environmental schemes which would come with Park designation plus Ranger services. Small businesses, particularly those linked to tourism, foresaw an increase in trade and economic viability as visitors were attracted to the new areas. Towns such as Kirby Stephen and Tebay realised they had much to gain from an influx of visitors wishing to stay in the area or stop for refreshment.

Opposition mainly came from a few landowners in the Lune Valley and local politicians in some District or County Councils. Just as their predecessors in the old local authorities had bitterly opposed the new National Park in 1954 because it diluted their fiefdoms, so the arguments were once again used about lack of local accountability and democracy, even though in reality locally elected representatives would retain the overall majority in any planning committee. In fact 'local' representation is always a relative term, especially in huge counties like North Yorkshire and Cumbria where elected representatives may live and be elected by voters 50 or more miles away from the individual making a planning application.

The most emotional and potentially divisive issue was the proud name 'Yorkshire', which was clearly inapplicable, not so much in those areas of the National Park such as Dent, Garsdale and Sedbergh that historically had been part of the old West Riding of Yorkshire, but in areas such as the Lune Valley, Mallerstang and, above all, the villages within the Orton Fells. In the former Westmorland the concern was they would now lose something of their identity if included in the Yorkshire Dales National Park. Worst of all was when it was mischievously suggested that the name 'Yorkshire' would have to be dropped from the Dales National Park. The popular press and attention-seeking politicians were soon quick to capture some easy and inevitably negative headlines in local papers and on regional television.

Supporters of the boundary changes were quick to point out that what mattered was to protect the areas against such unpopular threats as Wind Farms – with one proposal already being mooted for the shoulders of Wild Boar Fell before designation. It was suggested it would be better to discuss any possible changes to the name at a future date. One suggestion not yet entirely dismissed is to bring back the historic and much loved name of Westmorland and to refer to the new National Park as the Yorkshire Dales and Westmorland Fells National Park. This would keep everyone happy. The Yorkshire Dales would remain, as it must as an international brand for those areas which are truly in historic Yorkshire, and the old name Westmorland would be revived. The National Park Authority is, after all, a bureaucracy and the areas themselves will keep the names that people actually use, not what officials decide.

Given the overwhelming support for the proposals arising out of consultation, in 2012 Natural England decided to go ahead with the proposal and the Yorkshire Dales National Park Variation Order was published.

Predictably objections were received from some local authorities, and as a result in June 2013 a Public Inquiry took place in Kendal on both the Lakes and the Dales Orders. As well as the FLD/YDS Key Supporters Group evidence, and national bodies such as the Campaign for National Parks, CPRE, the Ramblers, British Mountaineering Council and other outdoor and amenity groups, there was support from Parish Councils, landowners, farmers and local businesses. The Inquiry, conducted by Inspector Roy Foster, was deliberately non-confrontational , and focused on the single issue of the suitability of the areas within the new boundary extension of both National Parks for designation, not on side issues such as the name of the expanded Park Authorities.

The Inquiry lasted for just five days and in the autumn of 2013 the Inspector submitted his report to the Secretary of State for his consideration. It was hoped that a decision would be given early in 2014.

If approved, the Yorkshire Dales National Park will increase in size from 1,762 to 2,165 square kilometres, becoming approximately 20 per cent larger in size, making it one of the largest UK National Parks. There would be some serious issues to be resolved including governance, with new representatives needed from Cumbria County and Eden District (Cumbria changing from covering 12% to 27% of the Park's area), which may have implications for the number of representatives of North Yorkshire and the other Districts on the Authority, including on the politically sensitive Planning Committee. For the first time the National Park would include a small part of Lancashire (less than one per cent), reflecting the importance of natural beauty and not administrative boundaries in the designation.

There will be rather more serious issues still to resolve. Additional finance will be required from central Government to deal with the larger area and various additional duties. It is estimated that the new responsibilities will require a further £500,000 per annum in addition to the Authority's current £4.2 million annual budget. There are also such matters as the management of rights of way and green lanes to resolve between Cumbria County Council and Lancashire County Council, as well as taking on new responsibilities for landowner and farm liaison and Ranger services, plus other visitor management and issues. New partnerships will have to be developed, new ideas shared. The Yorkshire Dales will become a different National Park, with new opportunities, new areas to be discovered and interpreted, and new traditions to explore.

It will be a rewarding challenge. Whether or not sufficient resources will actually be made available to meet that challenge is a matter still to be determined. At the time of writing, we first await the Secretary of State's decision on whether to confirm the legal Orders for these magnificent areas.

Much of the remarkable landscape of the Yorkshire Dales has changed little down the years, as epitomised by this view looking over limestone outcrops to the distinctive shape of Penyghent. (Bruce Rollinson –YPN)

Chapter Ten

The Future of the Yorkshire Dales National Park

If you were to go back 60 years to look at the landscape of the Yorkshire Dales, one criterion for success of the National Park over that period of time is perhaps how little that remarkable landscape has apparently changed, when so many parts of urban Britain are now unrecognisable compared with the 1950s, with massive new highways, car parks, supermarkets, high rise office blocks and demolition of formerly familiar older buildings.

And indeed if you look at the old photographs, superficially this is true. The majestic forms of Ingleborough and Penyghent look as much as they did in 1954, as does Malham Cove, Aysgarth Falls or the slender Gothic arches of Bolton Priory by the timeless River Wharfe.

One of the most important achievements of the National Park is reflected in all the many things that didn't happen. There are no huge new quarries blighting the landscape (in fact only four working quarries now remain in the National Park and all have a finite life). Intrusive new roads were not built across the Park apart from the two improved quarry

The Yorkshire Dales Millennium Trust plants its one-millionth tree at Calm Slate Wood on the Bolton Abbey Estate. Wielding the spades are the actor Simon Rouse; David Sharrod, Director of YDMT; and Phil Richards, National Park Area Ranger for Lower Wharfedale. (Phil Richards – YDMT)

Village shops have frequently closed or changed out of all recognition. This photograph of a well-stocked and traditional shop at Austwick dates from about 1959. (W R Mitchell)

access roads between Swinden Quarry and Skipton and Horton and Settle in Upper Ribblesdale. We haven't had any ghastly new theme parks and holiday home estates, though one or two of the larger caravan sites have expanded and morphed into villages of permanent homes. Villages have not been swamped with rings of new executive homes and retirement bungalows as has happened around many towns and villages outside the National Park. There has only been one major new reservoir scheme, at Grimwith, and most people would concede this was so well

planned that it has enhanced the landscape and its biodiversity. Major commercial afforestation schemes were limited to the top end of Langstrothdale and whilst their timber extraction is now causing problems long term, there will be environmental gains. The green lanes are now protected from over-use by motor vehicles.

Look more closely at those old photographs and you'll actually see a lot more trees in the landscape. Whilst the Yorkshire Dales was noted as having barely 4% of its denuded landscapes covered by trees, much

Many village schools have also closed, but a happy survivor is this delightful building at Burnsall which has hardly changed in the last 300 years. It is seen here in the late 1950s. (Bertram Unné)

This photograph of some wonderful autumn tints at Bolton Abbey is relatively recent, but the slender arches of the Priory look very much as they did in 1954 – and much earlier. (Bruce Rollinson – YPN)

Filming in Settle of the award winning *Lad: A Yorkshire Story*. In this scene the aggrieved son of a Dales quarry worker is about to spray the 'Allied Bank' with a good dose of farmyard manure! (YDMT)

more native amenity woodland has now appeared. The Yorkshire Dales Millennium Trust recently planted its one-millionth tree (not all of these were of course within the National Park). The long-running Dales Woodland Restoration Programme, which is delivered and funded by a partnership of the YDMT, Yorkshire Dales National Park Authority and the Forestry Commission, continues to fund and support farmers and landowners. This enables them to undertake many excellent tree-planting projects, mainly in gills and hillsides in ways that enhance both landscape quality and biodiversity. There have been other worthwhile tree planting projects such as work by the Woodland Trust and private landlords and estate managers using a variety of grant schemes.

Many of the characteristic barns and drystone

walls in prime areas of the Dales such as in Upper Swaledale, Upper Wharfedale and Littondale are now in a pristine condition, thanks to highly successful schemes such as the Park's Barns and Walls initiative, and the Millennium Trust's Environet project. However at the fringes you'll see plenty of areas on the higher and lonelier hillsides where walls have tumbled, barns and even farmsteads have become ruined, with reed infested slopes where 60 years ago were green pastures. With less manpower available on Dales farms, walls and barns that no longer have a stock keeping and boundary function are not a priority.

But what of the villages, and the communities that live in them? Again it is a complex picture. Superficially, villages and hamlets have never looked better or more prosperous. Even humble farmworkers' or even former miners' cottages are now carefully restored, with neatly tended gardens, either as someone's dream retirement home or a weekend or holiday cottage. Once derelict barns and outbuildings in villages such as Grassington or Reeth have been converted to homes and apartments, whilst rather uniform local authority housing – once pejoratively termed Council Houses – now have all the added sparkle of owner-occupier property improvement.

On one level Dales communities are thriving. Coming to live in a typical larger Dales village is a bit like joining a rather nice social club. Networks of neighbours and friendships provide support, absent from the impersonal suburbs of a city, and there are countless societies, church and other groups offering countless coffee mornings, talks, quizzes, trips, and activities. The village hall will still be a focus of activity, whether a drama group or fitness class. The energetic and active newly retired, including many people with professional backgrounds, provide the energy and initiative to make things happen and get things done.

The village shop and post office in all but the larger villages may have closed, as have many village schools (others are threatened) but unlike in other rural areas, the pub will have probably survived mainly because of the influx of visitors at weekends and

Kit Calvert, a noted dalesman who established the Wensleydale Creamery in Hawes. (David Joy collection)

holiday times buying food and drink. Even where there are fewer visitors in places such as Carleton in Coverdale and Hudswell above Swaledale, social enterprises have been established within the village to buy the pub and employ tenant staff to keep it as the focal point of social activity.

The real change over the last 60 years however has been the loss of working families and their children. With farming requiring far less semi-skilled labour, quarries being reduced in number and now more highly mechanised, and loss of the last few small manufactories, less workers are needed. Even quarry wagon drivers tend to come from outside the area. There is little or no manufacturing or industry in the National Park – 60 years ago there were still one or two working mills, a cardboard making factory in Ribblesdale.

The Wensleydale Creamery in Hawes is however

a notable and worthy exception. Originally established by the legendary Kit Calvert in the 1930s to help Dales farmers by manufacturing and marketing Wensleydale cheese, when Dairy Crest, a subsidiary of the Milk Marketing Board, closed it down in 1992 with the loss of 59 local jobs, a local buy-out and its reopening as an independent company proved a huge success story. The Creamery now employs 190 local people and collects milk from 36 local dairy farms. Part of the success of this project lies in the fact that, in the centre of the National Park, it is also a major all-year, all-weather visitor attraction, where visitors can see the famous cheese being made, take home a sample as well as enjoying a meal – with or without one of the specialist cheeses – in the restaurant.

But in other parts of the Dales the position is much bleaker, for young people in particular. With loss of the kind of semi-skilled jobs which would allow young people to start as an apprentice or shop floor assistant to work their way up to becoming a skilled operator and eventually a manager, many younger people born in the Dales have no option but to leave the area for work.

Nowhere is this situation better explored than in the award-winning film *Lad: A Yorkshire Story* written and directed by local author Dan Hartley, released in 2012 and filmed in Ribblesdale. It explores the anger and despair of a son of a Dales quarry worker whose brother has to join the army to find work and whose family face eviction after the sudden death of his father. It is the beautifully explored relationship between a teenage boy, Tom Proctor, and a National Park Ranger that brings the lad to maturity and acceptance. Although the film offers no easy solution to the dilemma of young people leaving the area, the fact that Tom learns self-discipline and training through conservation work offers a hope for the future not only for young people but the National Park.

Conservation and protection of a great cultural landscapes such as the Yorkshire Dales can and will only happen if there are enough people available and engaged with the skill and dedication needed to rebuild the walls and barns, to restore the historic buildings, to plant the trees and ensure woodland remains stock and pest proof, to reseed the meadows with native wild flowers, to ensure that the great grouse moors of the eastern uplands not only retain their beauty but add to their biodiversity and peatland carbon capture.

Such things will not happen purely as a result of market forces. There has to be external funding in whatever form which, like the Millennium Environet programme and various Heritage Lottery and EU-Leader fund projects, can also bring in considerable amounts of private sector match funding. Such funding creates jobs which in turn act as an economic multiplier in Dales communities as young wage earners spend money on food, accommodation, supplies and living costs. But to participate requires a skilled labour force, enough younger people with at least basic levels of skill who can work alongside experienced craftsmen and women who, like the Ranger Al in *Lad*, can pass on their skills and knowledge and love of the Dales to this next generation.

There have been a number of worthwhile apprenticeship and training schemes designed to give young people skills and experience in such areas as environmental conservation, stonewalling and traditional buildings, forestry, horticulture and even gamekeeping and butchery, to allow them to reach a level where they can work with skilled craftsmen and women, developing the specialist skills needed. An example is the *Dales Rural Trainee Scheme* managed by the Yorkshire Dales Millennium Trust in partnership with Craven, Askham Bryan and Newton Rigg Colleges. This scheme allows up to ten local young people to be offered apprenticeships, giving them the experience and skill needed to work for the kind of small specialist companies which are able to deliver on a range of landscape conservation and related projects.

Two major hurdles hindering young people aspiring to return to work in the Dales relate to both housing and transport. Lack of affordable local housing has been a continuous problem in the Dales. The National Park as planning authority has developed sometimes controversial policies to ensure

'Abandoned Landscape'

'Wilderness Landscape'

Paintings by Hannah Chesterman captured the kind of future foreseen for the National Park in the Landscapes for Tomorrow project.

'Sporting Landscape'

'Conserved Landscape'

that new housing in the National Park should be prioritised for local need rather than being available on the open market, as affluent outsiders can always outbid local families. The National Park Authority is not, however, the local housing authority, and whilst various schemes such as housing associations and shared equity have developed many worthwhile projects, notably for sheltered accommodation for older people, relatively little is available for young local families.

The selling off of local authority housing and the resultant lack of property at affordable rents has forced many people on low or even average salaries, even when they have found jobs in the Dales, to live outside the area and to commute into the Dales – if the job pays enough to own and run a car as public transport in the Dales is often skeletal in nature, especially early and late in the day. Catering and hotel workers are especially vulnerable to high transport and living costs which explains why many pubs and restaurants in the Dales are staffed by young East Europeans without family commitments who are prepared to work antisocial hours and use sparse 'live-in' accommodation which allows them to save money when they return to Poland or Slovakia to pursue higher education or more lucrative careers.

There could be solutions which might, however, pose challenges to the National Park as a planning authority. Radical designs of wooden framed, prefabricated zero-carbon 'passive houses', using green technology developed in Germany, are being pioneered in Pembrokeshire and elsewhere, costing as little as £50,000 per unit, but at the moment would not meet traditional ideas of stone built cottages to meet National Park policy requirements and which are well outside the price range of working families in the Dales.

But how has the National Park Authority itself changed over those 60 years? It was not of course an independent authority until 1997, only a committee of North Yorkshire County Council and prior to 1974 two subcommittees of the two County Councils. In the early years the 'National Park' was little more than a line on a map and various policies, which may have seemed excellent in intention, lacked resources to enforce or deliver and were little more than pious intentions.

For good and for ill, the National Park's role as Local Planning Authority, whilst essential in preventing the despoliation of the Park by unsuitable and unsightly development, was, is and will always remain controversial, deeply unpopular with certain sections of the local community, especially people with land and property to develop for whom planning is too often perceived as a restriction on their personal freedom. The very name 'Authority' is something that raises instinctive hackles among the very independent minded communities of the Dales.

Apart from a few information centres, car parks, toilets and National Park Wardens with their familiar Land Rovers, in the early years little actually happened on the ground. Preventing local people and businesses doing things through planning controls appeared to be merely negative. There were too few positive things to see. Only when Park budgets were significantly increased after 1974, did more popular things start to happen, with action in areas such as rights of way, the purchase of an Outdoor Centre, the groundbreaking Dales Rail scheme, and a much extended range of interpretive publications, guided walks programmes and a far higher profile for the Ranger service and for Dales Volunteers.

The setting up, by the National Park Authority, of the independent Yorkshire Dales Millennium Trust was a masterstroke. The Authority devoted considerable financial and staff resource time, including initially the salary of its first Director Richard Witt, as a way of bringing in new human and financial resources into the National Park to deliver major benefits and realise many key National Park objectives. This could never have happened under the hawkish regime of various Treasury Ministers and civil servants for whom public spending by National Parks has always been, and remains, an easy target for career boosting cost savings.

From 1997 onwards there has been a fundamental cultural shift, especially under the chairmanships of Robert Heseltine, Steve Macaré and Carl Lis. Playing a key role was Heather Hancock, who in 1998 became the Authority's Chief Executive Officer and the first woman in the country to hold such a position. David Butterworth, her successor and the current holder of the post, has built on her initial work. The idea of a National Park being an all-powerful controlling body that decides and delivers what was in the National Park Plan is basically obsolete. The Park Authority has been transformed to becoming an enabling body, a facilitator, working with a range of partners to deliver key National Park objectives, those objectives also agreed with those partners who include the local community.

To some extent this approach came out of necessity, as after every short burst of revenue increase from central Government there came a period of retrenchment, with a real risk that with a larger staff and even larger overheads, there would be no budgets to deliver any actual project work, as budgets were frozen or totally cut. But by seeking out partners with common objectives and interest in the National Park, including public agencies such as Natural England, the Environment Agency, English Heritage, statutory authorities such as the Water Companies, the energy companies, Network Rail, voluntary bodies such as the National Trust, RSPB and Wildlife Trusts, and of course the Millennium Trust, but above all private landowners, grouse moor owners, foresters and farmers, the National Park has been able to deliver many projects such as Limestone Country or the Dales Tourism Business Partnership it could not have delivered alone. By working together to share common objectives not only can funding and personnel be shared, but new insights and skills can be combined and new ideas brought forward. The Park's Management Plan now lists key delivery partners for all its core policy objectives.

So what kind of future lies ahead for this very different kind of National Park? This question was debated in 1989 through an imaginative project which looked at several scenarios for the future. Known as *Landscapes for Tomorrow,* the project was run by the University of East Anglia in partnership with the National Park and Social Research Council under the direction of Professor Tim O'Riordan. He and the late Dr Chris Wood of the Yorkshire Dales National Park were assisted by Ann Shadrake,

Research Associate. An elaborate board game was devised to get participants to make choices about what kind of landscape they foresaw and would choose for the Dales. These choices were transformed into paintings by the artist Hannah Chesterman to give an impression of what the National Park might look like in decades ahead. The Dales could become, for example, an 'Abandoned Landscape' which suggests what the Dales would look like if hill farming lost all public intervention and farms went out of business, and much unused farmland became overgrown with scrub, or a 'Wilderness Landscape' if large amounts of land were set aside for nature conservation and amenity woodland, or a 'Sporting Landscape' if commercial shooting, riding and hunting interests became the main land use. The favoured option was what was later termed the 'Conserved Landscape', which relied on very large public subsidies to pay farmers to continue traditional methods that favoured diversification and conserved the drystone walls and barns. This would keep a landscape which, whilst it would continue to change, would be broadly that of the pastoral landscape of the late 20th century, whilst increasing biodiversity with, for example, more native woodland on the eroded uplands.

What *Landscapes for Tomorrow* implied is that we do, as a society, have choices about the future countryside we'd like to live in. It is not a matter of allowing market forces unrestricted freedom to destroy and exploit, but intervene in various ways that society chooses, to create the kind of landscape we wish to see. That is ultimately what a National Park could mean for the mid-late 21st century – the next 60 years.

But given continued cuts in public sector funding how can this be achieved? Even when it has little money to put on the table the National Park can still make things happen. The financial crash of 2008 and consequent austerity cuts to all local authority and public sector funding have caused the National Park Authority to lose around a third of its staff. Fortunately front line services were, wherever possible, protected, with the Ranger Service, albeit with some slimming down, being still there to

The awe-inspiring chasm of Gordale Scar is one of the many glories of the Yorkshire Dales National Park. (Bruce Rollinson – YPN)

Less spectacular than the limestone scenery but just as wonderful in their way are the meadow flowers of the Dales. (Pippa Rayner – YDMT)

The well-maintained rights of way network is a major factor in attracting tourists to the Yorkshire Dales. Symbolising the opportunities is this signpost pointing the way towards Wharfe, near Austwick. (Beverley Middleton)

protect rights of way and access matters, and to work with farmers and landowners to resolve visitor management issues. The Dales Volunteers, a group which evolved from the old National Park Voluntary Warden scheme, now has around 250 members from all walks of life. Their work which has helped to complement, but not replace, the work of professional staff, includes providing leaders for guided walks and events, carrying out access, heritage and archaeological surveys for the Authority, undertaking practical conservation work on footpaths and in Nature Reserves, giving talks and demonstrations, and in every way acting as ambassadors for the National Park.

Other voluntary groups such as the Yorkshire Dales Society also offer support in various ways, most notably with its Dales & Bowland CIC taking responsibility for the National Park's remarkable Sunday DalesBus network. Acting as a catalyst for voluntary sector contribution for both conservation work and visitor management activity, especially interpretation and education, will be a key role for the National Park in the future.

National Parks because of their landscape quality and high visitor profile also offer individuals and groups alternative lifestyle choices, whether these lie in running a design company, an IT consultancy or devoting a life to self-sufficient, permaculture hill farming in the heart of the Dales, or developing a specialist practice in renewable energy installation. Rather than the National Park and its visitors being a restriction to the future of hill farming, a combination of whatever agri-environmental schemes the future may bring, artisan food production such as beef, high quality sausages, sheep cheese, or maybe comfortable bed and breakfast or self-catering accommodation in a converted barn on the farm, or perhaps a combination of all these enterprise-led activities, could enable a working Dales family to stay in business and prosper. It is such people who will be the true guardians of the landscape and culture of the Yorkshire Dales, not only in the immediate future, but in the decades to come.

In 2008 the Yorkshire Dales National Park Authority and Nidderdale Area of Outstanding Natural Beauty JAC were awarded the Europarc Charter for Sustainable Tourism, which was renewed in 2013. Sustainable tourism is about small scale, localised visitor activity respecting the unique qualities of an environment, walking, cycling or using a local bus rather than driving, staying locally, eating local food, buying local products, respecting and sharing local culture and helping to sustain the local economy. Studies show that more income from this kind of 'sensitive' tourism activity stays within the local economy. But it must also be business-led, driven by people with a passion and love for the Dales and its environment, who choose to run a small business to help them to share their love and enjoyment of the area and its distinctive landscape and culture.

The Charter and its development has given the Park Authority a new focus on the role of small businesses, directly and indirectly linked to tourism, to help create the wealth to sustain the landscape. Small and medium sized businesses, which include farming enterprises, are key to keeping the Dales a living landscape. Their success will prevent the Dales from becoming a ghetto of the elderly and wealthy, as small enterprises not only need to employ people, but can also attract the likes of the fictional Tom Proctor, who perhaps by his thirties might have a degree in (say) environmental management, might return to his native Ribblesdale to open and run a small business linked to one or more or future agri-environmental schemes. He would be helped by having access to the new networks of Superfast Broadband that can enable a business to be run from almost anywhere in the world. Why live in a congested and polluted city if you can run your business from and within the stunning landscape of a National Park? Of if you were a young person with different strengths and abilities, maybe you come back to the Dales to work for a drystone waller or building restoration company – if indeed you can find somewhere to live at a rent that is not geared to the inflated property prices of South East England.

A report in 2006 for the Campaign for National Parks *Prosperity and Parks* reported that in the two and a quarter National Parks in the Yorkshire & Humber

Region – the Dales, Moors and part of the Peak District – businesses in those Parks generated £1.8 billion and 34,000 jobs, with 65% of business consulted reporting that the special environment of the National Park contributed to their success. Employment levels were better in areas within the National Park than outside, giving lie to the old myth that National Park designation restricts economic growth. The very reverse is true. A 2013 study undertaken on behalf of the English National Park Authorities also concluded that English National Parks contribute between £4.1 and £6.3 billion to the UK economy through business activity within their boundaries – the equivalent of the entire UK aerospace industry.

Impressive as these figures are, this growing economic success will depend on the continued existence of a strong well-funded National Park Authority at its heart to co-ordinate and champion support for such enterprise, at national and regional level, to enable them to succeed, and to support the core environmental infrastructure which is essential for that success. One interesting statistic underlines this point. A study by consultants Ecotec in 2003 discovered that 90% of the value of tourism in the Yorkshire Dales is based around an accessible, well maintained rights of way network. As the disaster of the Foot and Mouth epidemic revealed in 2001, if that access is not available, visitors will not come. The National Park Authority currently spends around £400,000 per annum – around 10% of its annual budget – maintaining and improving its 2000km rights of way network. Take that core infrastructure funding away and the tourist industry in the Dales would rapidly decline and eventually collapse.

At no time since the Second World War has Britain faced a more challenging and uncertain future. This includes global economic problems caused by climate change and its impact on world prices if crops fail or political disruption occurs, and economic uncertainty as the emerging super powers of East Asia in particular overtake Europe in an increasingly challenging and destructive race for the world's declining natural resources.

There is real fear that a Government determined to 'roll back the state' with massive further cuts to public sector funding over the next five years to such non protected areas as transport (outside London), the environment and the arts, could reach levels which threaten the entire future of National Parks in Britain. By 2018 the Yorkshire Dales Park could be reduced to its core development control and planning functions, returning to the early years of the National Park when little or nothing actually happened on the ground because of lack of resources. Such cuts will make a microscopic difference to the overall national balance of payments, yet would cost the country in lost earnings and wealth creation far more than they actually save.

What Britain can offer the world is a remarkable cultural heritage which includes the great landscapes of its National Parks which are as important and attractive to overseas visitors as its historic buildings, its art and architecture, its rich literary and musical heritage. Even to the most philistine, costcutting bureaucrat, the potential economic value of the Yorkshire Dales National Park in generating cash from elsewhere in the UK and especially from overseas to support our balance of payments is immense.

But it's not just a question of pound notes. National Parks also embody deeply held spiritual values. It was the great Romantic poets, novelists, painters such as Wordsworth, Shelley, Keats, Byron, Hardy, Emily Bronte, Cotman, Constable, Turner, Ruskin and their many later disciplines who were inspired by the landscape of our island. Their work in turn inspired the social reformers who realised the immense potential of great landscape and open spaces to inspire people of all ages, to give them new meaning and purpose in life, to improve their physical and mental health and well-being. Visionaries like John Ruskin who taught us the value of natural beauty in both art and architecture, Octavia Hill one of the founders of the National Trust, Arthur Leonard who created both the CHA and Holiday Fellowship, Tom Stephenson creator of the Pennine Way and his friend John Dower, all helped shape our understanding of what a National Park such as the Yorkshire Dales should be and what

The National Park has some of the finest limestone pavement in Britain – and looks at its best when it has the distinctive shape of Ingleborough in the background. (Welcome to Yorkshire)

it can do for the quality of all our lives.

In a similar period of quite astonishing change to our own, the teaching of the great Romantic thinkers of the late 18th and early 19th centuries has never been more relevant or urgent. Just as they urged us to return to nature in the first Industrial Revolution, the message is equally valid in the Cybernetic Revolution of the 21st century.

Technology itself – especially the intensity and rapidity of changes in communication technology – provides huge benefits to humanity in terms of instant communication between individuals and institutions in ways which even a few short years ago would have seemed inconceivable. We can literally write, speak, and even see across great distances in seconds, in ways which literally shrink both time and space. In the comfort of our homes we can not only speak to, but see each other through a screen in ways which previous generations would have believed to be miraculous. The power of internet search engines to put huge libraries of information at our finger tips gives us enormous power. Research that once would have taken years with constant visits to distant libraries can now be accomplished in moments. The implications of this new power are enormous.

But there is a less welcome, a darker side. Virtual reality can too easily take on a life of its own. When image and reality are blurred there are dangers. Information technology has the power to take us into an obsessive, internalised virtual world. Why walk or cycle in a cold, wet and windy National Park when you can watch a carefully sanitised version on a screen or even on specially adapted cyber spectacles?

Yet the education value of the National Park, a way of reconnecting us with the real, the concrete, the actual, natural world in which we as sentient, living creatures exist and survive, is immense. The Yorkshire Dales National Park is at one and the same time a huge outdoor classroom and research laboratory. Where else in Britain can you see finer examples of limestone pavement or glacial erratics, better study the genetic diversity of a herb rich meadow, examine the early origins of Bronze Age farming or the industrial revolution? Malham Tarn Field Studies Centre, in a National Nature Reserve,

is nationally known for its research and teaching of subjects, from archaeology, entomology and plant ecology to the historic patterns of climate change and their influence on our environment. But this work focuses on the external environment of the Dales landscape as its core resource. This in turn is dependent on the area's continued protection from damaging development and active measures for its conservation.

The National Park's own amazing website *Out of Oblivion – a Landscape Through Time* gives access to a huge range of material about the evolving historic landscape that is the Yorkshire Dales, but underpinning that is the protection and conservation of that archaeology and historic environment, and access to it in both intellectual and physical terms. This is something that a well-resourced, multi-disciplinary National Park Authority can uniquely enable.

But there is another vital reason for National Parks to thrive. Britain is becoming an increasingly unequal society, one entirely dominated by a single city-region, London, almost a state within a state, with people enjoying salaries, bonuses and wealth beyond the wildest dreams of most people living in the rest of England. There is a real risk that like it did for the 18th century merchant bankers and the 19th century industrialists, this new wealth will result in the emergence of a new superclass able to buy farmland or moorland to convert it into just the kind of exclusive sporting estates envisaged in *Landscapes for Tomorrow*. The weakening of planning regulations could lead to conversion of traditional farms and even barns to luxury mansions and paddocks, the closure of rights of way and public access in a return to pre-industrial ideas of property rights and countryside for the privileged and powerful, most of which was closed off to all but the few.

National Parks remain as a powerful mechanism to safeguard personal freedom and choice, our human right to access and enjoy a shared inheritance, an inheritance that must at all costs be protected and defended for future generations.

In essence, National Parks are about people – people who live and work in these magnificent landscapes and who benefit from their surroundings, and people whose lives are enriched, by being able to access those same landscapes for spiritual renewal, inspiration and health giving outdoor exercise. In turn those visitors support the local economy on which the local communities depend.

Even if you are poor, you can walk, cycle or perhaps catch one of the remaining bus services into the Yorkshire Dales, climb to the summit of Ingleborough to enjoy that magnificent sweep of open fells and distant shoreline, walk into the awe-inspiring limestone chasm of Gordale, stroll through the flower meadows of Swaledale, amble through Strid Woods in the gold and crimson glory of late autumn, see the pale winter sunshine glisten off the frozen surface of Semerwater, or wander along the Dales Way in Dentdale as the first primroses unfold in hedgerows and riverside.

The Yorkshire Dales is part of everyone's birthright, no matter where we were born, our ethnic origin or income. That is the true meaning of the word 'National' in the name Yorkshire Dales National Park.

The century or so of campaigning that led to the establishment and properly funded and resourced National Parks must not be allowed to be destroyed by shortsighted cuts by Whitehall officials who neither understand nor care about what happens outside the charmed ring of the M25, least of all the importance of investment in its infrastructure which includes our National Parks, five of which are in the North. There could not be a stronger case of devolving funding decisions to the Regions, and to the North of England in particular.

Ultimately, we live in a democracy, and as citizens of that democracy we have the power to ensure that the Yorkshire Dales National Park does not suffer death by a thousand cuts, slow starvation as the lifeblood of investment and finance is slowly strangled to leave the patient weakened and finally lifeless. Both as individuals and through such organisations as the Yorkshire Dales Society, the Campaign for National Parks, CPRE, the Ramblers, and through more local bodies such as wildlife trusts and parish councils, we can and must make our voice, the voice of the majority, heard, loudly and clearly to ensure Government, both locally and nationally, realises the need to safeguard all our National Parks, including the Yorkshire Dales.

The story of the Yorkshire Dales National Park over the last sixty years is a remarkable one, something to be both proud of and to celebrate. It was established when Britain was still emerging from the economic impacts of a horrific war. We were a much poorer nation yet its leaders had ambitious priorities for our people, even if it took another six decades fully to realise that vision in terms of the Yorkshire Dales National Park.

The challenge for all of us is to ensure that this vision is recaptured, not in precisely the same way as in the past – we are now a different people living in a different society – but in ways which are relevant for the coming years of the 21st century. Economic change worldwide may indeed result in Britain becoming, in crude material terms, a poorer society, but in terms of spiritual values, as well as better physical and mental health, and wellbeing, a far richer and happier one.

The Yorkshire Dales National Park will be there as a continuing inspiration, to enable such a transformation to happen.

Snow gives a new dimension to the limestone pavement, Ingleborough – and the stunted hawthorn tree. (Sara Spillett)

Acknowledgements

This book could not have been written without the invaluable help of many people – Ray Woolmore whose history of the National Park's designation process is masterly, David Butterworth and Kathryn Beardmore of the National Park Authority, David Vose of Natural England, David Sharrod, Don Gamble and colleagues at the Yorkshire Dales Millennium Trust, Ann Shadrake of the Yorkshire Dales Society, my co-author Anthony Bradley with his excellent chapter on the changes to farming over the last 60 years, but above all from my editor, David Joy who is also responsible for the illustrations that make the text come alive.

Needless to say, any mistakes or errors of fact are entirely my own.

Finally, as always, to Fleur, whose support, advice and sharing of ideas and experience, lie at the heart of what this book is about.

Further information

The Yorkshire Dales National Park Authority,
Colvend, Hebden Road, Grassington, North Yorkshire, BD23 5LB.
01756 751600
www.yorkshiredales.org.uk

The Yorkshire Dales Millennium Trust,
Old Post Office, Main Street, Clapham, North Yorkshire, LA2 8DP.
015242 51002
www.ydmt.org

The Yorkshire Dales Society,
Canal Wharf, Eshton Road, Gargrave, North Yorkshire, BD23 3PN.
01756 749400
www.yds.org.uk

Select Bibliography

Abbott, Stan & Whitehouse, Alan: *The Line that Refused to Die* (Leading Edge Press 1990).

Council for National Parks: *National Parks for Life: An Agenda for Action* (CNP 1997).

Council for National Parks: *Prosperity and Protection – The Economic Impact of National Parks in the Yorkshire & Humber Region* (CNP 2006).

Countryside Commission: *Dales Rail – A report of an experimental project in the Yorkshire Dales National Park* (C120 Countryside Commission 1979)

DEFRA: *National Park Authorities – Assessment of Benefits* (Working Paper – DEFRA 2011).

Dower, John: *National Parks in England and Wales* (HMSO 1945).

Gamble, Don & St Pierre, Tanya: *Hay Time in the Yorkshire Dales* (Scotforth Books Lancaster 2010).

Hartley, Marie & Ingilby, Joan: *The Yorkshire Dales* (Dent 1963).

Lee, Frank: *Cumbria's Forgotten Landscapes* (Friends of the Lake District 2005).

Mitchell, W.R.: *The Story of the Yorkshire Dales* (Philimore 1999).

North Yorkshire County Council Yorkshire Dales National Park Committee: *An Advisory Hierarchy of Roads for the Yorkshire Dales National Park* (NYCC 1981).

Poore, Duncan & Judy: *Protected Landscapes – the United Kingdom Experience* (Countryside Commission et al 1987).

Raistrick, Arthur: *Pennine Walls* (Dalesman 1946).

Raistrick, Arthur: *The making of the English Landscape – West Riding of Yorkshire* (Hodder & Stoughton 1970).

Ramblers Association: *Ramblers News* (quarterly journal 1949-1959).

Rubinstein, David & Speakman, Colin: *Leisure, Transport and the Countryside* (Fabian Research Series pamphlet 277 1969).

Simmons I.G. (Editor): *Yorkshire Dales – National Park Guide No 9* (HMSO 1971).

Singleton, Andy & Joy, David: *Barns of the Yorkshire Dales* (Great Northern 2008).

Speakman, Colin: *Yorkshire Dales – the Official National Park Guide* (Pevensey 2001).

Speakman, Colin: *Walk! A Celebration of Striding Out* (Great Northern 2011).

Towler, James: *The Battle for the Settle & Carlisle* (Platform 5 1990).

Waltham, Tony: *Yorkshire Dales National Park Official Guide* (Webb & Bower 1987).

White, Robert: *The Yorkshire Dales – A Landscape Through Time* (Great Northern 2005).

Woolmore Ray: *Designation History Series – Yorkshire Dales National Park* (Countryside Agency 2002).

Wright Geoffrey N.: *Roads and Trackways of the Yorkshire Dales* (Moorland 1985).

Other significant sources include various Annual Reports and Committee Minutes and papers and websites of the Yorkshire Dales National Park Committee (1974-1997), Yorkshire Dales National Park Authority (1997-present), Countryside Commission / Agency, Natural England, Yorkshire Dales Millennium Trust, Campaign for National Parks.

Index

Abercrombie, Patrick   10
Addison Committee   10
Advisory Road Hierarchy for the Dales   80, 81, 83
Afforestation   38, 39, 40, 99
Agricultural Development and Advisory Service (ADAS)   102
Aneorobic digesters   98
Area of Outstanding Natural Beauty   10
Aysgarth Falls   34, 117
Bainbridge – YDNP Offices   42
Baker, John   42, 50
Barden Moor & Fell Access Area   30, 32, 33, 34
Barker, Lawrence   34
Biofuel crops   99
Blenkinsop, Arthur   9, 31
Bolton Abbey   117, 120
Bovine Spongiform Encephalopathy (BSE)   66, 103
Brecon Beacons National Park   29
Bruntland Commission   50, 51

Calendar Girls   50
Calvert, Kit   122
Cam Fell Forest   39, 46, 99
Cam High Road   69, 71, 73, 74, 99
Campaign (Council) for National Parks   9, 47, 71, 83, 126, 135
Castle, Barbara   9
Chesterman, Hannah   127
Clapham Information Centre   32
Colvend Grassington NPA office   41
Cornish, Vaughan   10
Council for the Protection of Rural England (CPRE)   8, 47, 54, 80. 135
Country Landowners Association   54
Countryside & Rights of Way Act (CROW) Act 2000   51, 52, 70
Countryside Agency   10, 54, 110
Countryside Commission   10, 45, 54, 110
Countryside Holidays Association (CHA)   8
Countryside Stewardship/Agri-Agreements   63, 130
Coverdale   11
Craven District Council   41

Crossley, Norman   34
Cumbria County Council   39, 45, 74, 109, 115
Curtis, W. N.   12

Dales & Bowland Community Interest Company   86
Dales Access Forum   51, 53, 71
Dales Barns and Walls   56, 58 - 61, 63, 121, 122
Dales Bike Centre, Fremington   88
Dales Rail   81, 82, 83
Dales Volunteers / Voluntary Wardens   34, 43, 45, 130
Dales Way   39, 51, 135
DalesBus   84- 88, 130
Dalton, Hugh   12
Dartmoor National Park   29
Dentdale   10, 11, 46, 135
Development Control   42, 43, 123, 126
Dower, Arthur   30, 31, 47
Dower, John   8, 9, 10, 11, 30, 36, 110
Dower, Pauline   11, 47
Duke of Devonshire / Chatsworth Estate   31, 32, 41

Eden District Council   115
Education and training   43, 50, 52, 54, 64, 83, 123, 134
Embsay Railway (Bolton Abbey)   77, 79
Employment   122, 123, 130
Environment Act 1995   47, 50
Environment Agency   127
Environmentally Sensitive Areas (ESAs) / Stewardship   62, 63, 107
European Union / CAP Reform   62, 67, 84, 94, 99, 103, 106, 107
Exmoor National Park   10, 29

Farming   39, 46, 67, 99, 100 - 107.
Flowers of the Dales   66, 67, 128
Foot & Mouth Outbreak   50, 103. 106
Footpaths – Definitive Map / maintenance   10, 35, 43, 44, 46, 47, 69, 129
Forest of Bowland AONB   38, 54
Forestry Commission   38 , 121
Friends of DalesBus (Yorkshire Dales Public Transport Users Group)   84, 86

Friends of the Earth — 39, 94
Friends of the Lake District — 8, 110

Gamble, Don — 67
Go Dales Project — 47
Gordale — 24, 26, 46 128, 135
Grassington — 25,
Grassington Information Centre — 44
Grassington Moor — 91, 93
Greenfield Forest — 39
Ground source heat pumps — 95

Hallas, George — 42, 54
Hancock, Heather — 126
Hartley, Dan — 123
Hartley, Marie & Ingilby, Joan — 44, 58
Harvey, Richard — 41, 54
Hawes — 22, 29, 30
Hawes Dales Countryside museum — 44, 50, 58
Hay Meadows, Haytime — 16, 19, 21, 57, 63, 65, 66-7
Heseltine Robert — 54, 126
Hobhouse, Sir John — 9, 10, 11, 110
Holiday Fellowship (HF) — 8, 131
Holtby, Winifred — 31
Howgills — 10, 95 108, 109, 110, 112
Hydro electric schemes –Linton, Settle, Bainbridge,
Halton Gill — 97, 98

Ilkley Moor Rally — 31
Ingleborough National Nature Reserve — 28, 29, 132, 133
Ingleborough — 39, 132, 133

Joint Advisory Committee (Yorkshire Dales) 13, 30, 31, 36

Kielder Forest — 36

Lad: A Yorkshire Story — 121, 123
Lake District National Park — 10, 12, 29,
Lancashire County Council — 31, 115
Land Access & Recreation Association (LARA) 70, 71, 74, 75
Landscapes for Tomorrow — 124, 125, 127
Lee, Frank — 110
Limestone Country Project — 67, 127
Lis, Carl — 126
Local employment — 124
Local Government Act 1972 — 39
Local housing — 50, 123, 126
Local Sustainable Transport Fund — 86

Loch Lomond and the Trossachs National Park — 29
Lockwood, John — 34, 41
Lockyer, Keith — 41, 47
Long Distance Footpaths — 10

Macaré, Steve — 126
McEwan, Malcom — 50, 98
Macmillan, Harold — 10, 35
Malham Cove — 31, 32, 38, 46, 47, 48, 117
Malham Information Centre — 44
Malham Moor — 35, 36, 71, 75
Malham Youth Hostel — 36
Mallerstang — 109, 108, 110, 114
Mastiles Lane — 68, 71, 72, 74, 75, 81
Michael, Alun — 110
Milk Marketing Board / Milk Marque — 102, 103, 123
Mosaic Partnership (CNP) — 47, 86
Muir John — 8

National Cycle Network — 88
National Farmers' Union — 12
National Land Fund — 12
National Nature Reserves — 10, 28
National Park Committee North Riding — 30, 31, 34
National Park Committee West Riding — 30, 31, 32, 34
National Park Joint Planning Boards — 13, 30
National Park Plan / Local Plan / Management Plan
— 40, 42, 127
National Parks & Access to the Countryside Act 1949
— 9, 10, 29, 30, 35
National Parks Commission — 10, 31
National Trust — 8, 47, 48, 98, 127, 131
Natural England — 10, 54, 63, 66, 67, 110, 115127
New Forest National Park — 29, 111
Nidderdale AONB — 11, 12, 38, 54, 84, 130
North Pennines AONB — 74, 110
North Pennines Rural Development Board — 38, 39
North Riding of Yorkshire — 10, 13, 30, 31, 39
North York Moors National Park — 10, 29
North Yorkshire County Council — 39, 40, 42, 45, 46, 74, 86, 126

O'Riordan, Professor Tim — 127
Orton Fells — 110, 112

Passive House — 99, 126
Peak District National Park — 10, 11, 12, 30, 38
Pembrokeshire Coast National Park — 29, 126
Pennine Bridleway — 75

Pennine Motors 77
Pennine Way 27, 35, 36, 51
Pennines Dales ESA 62
Percival Brothers 76, 77
Perry Christa 66
Priestley, JB 39
Proctor, Wilf 32,33,34,41

Quarrying 31,37, 38. 117, 118

Raistrick, Arthur 9, 11, 13, 31
Ramblers Association 8, 31, 54,70,71, 135
Rayner, Pippa 66
Ribble Motor Services 77
Richmondshire District Council 41
Road Traffic Regulation Act 1984 74, 75
Roses Way Cycle link 88
Ryland, Andrew 84

Sandford Principle 73, 75
Sandys Duncan 3o
Scott Trial 69
Sedbergh 29, 30, 95, 110,114
Settle-Carlisle Railway 77, 81, 82,83,83, 91
Shadrake, Ann 127
Sharrod, David 54
Shevelan, Joe 34
Silkin, Lewis 9
Snowdonia National Park 10,29
Solar energy 92, 95, 98
South Lakeland District Council 41
South Yorkshire 39, 40
St Pierre, Tanya 67
Standing Committee on National Parks 9
Stephenson, Tom 9,31, 35, 109, 131
Stott, Roger 54
Sustainable Tourism 83, 130,131
Swaledale 10, 39, 57, 60, 76, 78, 94, 135

Three Peaks Project 36, 80, 82
Tour de France 88
Town and Country Planning Act 1947 7,27, 29
Townley, Lady Mary 75
Traffic in the Dales 38, 78, 79, 80, 82
Trail Riders Fellowship 69
Tree planting 54, 117, 118, 121

United Automobile Company 77, 78
Upland Management 62

Wainwright, Alfred 51, 109
Watson, Graham 47, 48
Wensleydale 12,13, 57, 78,94
Wensleydale Creamery, Hawes 122
Wensleydale Railway 12, 44, 76, 77,83, 84, 91
West Riding County Council 10, 11,12,30-31,36,38,39,40,41, 79, 14
West Yorkshire County Council 39,40, 86
West Yorkshire Road Car Co 77, 78
Whernside Manor, Dentdale 46
Wild Boar Fell 109, 111
Wildlife & Countryside Act 1981 62
Willey, Fred 9, 35
Williams, Louise 67
Wind turbines 94, 95, 96
Witt, Richard 54,126
Wood, Dr Chris 127
Woodland Trust 121
Wordsworth, William 8
Wright, Peter 34

Yellowstone National Park 8
York 30,39
Yorkshire Dales Cycle Way 88
Yorkshire Dales Green Lanes Advisory Group 74
Yorkshire Dales Green Lanes Alliance 71, 74, 75
Yorkshire Dales Millennium Trust 52, 53, 54,55,63,64, 117,121,126
Yorkshire Dales National Park Authority 47,50, 54, 71, 73, 75,84, 86, 98, 121, 126, 127, 135
Yorkshire Dales National Park Committee 40,41
Yorkshire Dales National Park Information Service 34,43, 47
Yorkshire Dales National Park Warden/Ranger service 34,41,43, 75, 127
Yorkshire Dales National Park 10,11, 12,40,43
Yorkshire Dales Railway – Skipton Grassington 79
Yorkshire Dales Society 46,47,54, 71, 86, 130
Yorkshire Wildlife Trust 66
Youth Hostels Association 8, 79

Subscribers

Rob Ackrel
Joan & Chris Alder
John and Claire Alderson
P C J Andrew
Joan Antcliff
Patrick Simon Arnold
James Ashton
Richard Bacon
David Bailey
Peter Balchin
David William Ball
William M Balmer
Prof Stephen Barnett
Mark Bashforth
The Beaumont Family
David K Beck
Derek Beeston
The Beetlestones, Ginnel Cottage
Dr A Belton
Shirley Bendon
Esther F Benson
Arthur J M Benson
Roger H Benson
Richard Bentley
Robin Benzie
Helen Bergman
Andrew Berriman
Phillip P Blades
Gill Bowen
Raymond F Bradford
Dr Keith Budd
Nigel M Burrow
Mr B Burton
Allan Butterfield
Dennis Cairns
Andrew Campbell
Ian Campbell
Richard Cant
Linda Capstick
Shirley Carmichael

Adam Carter
Samuel Case
Patricia Caudwell
Anne Chalkley
Hazel Chambers
M C & P Charlesworth
Christine Chisholm
C L Clarkson
Mr N J Clarkson
Perry Stephen Cliff
Cynthia Clifton
H B Clough
Jennifer Clough
Leslie Edward Cochrane
Peter D Colley
Anne Collins
John Collins
Valerie Cooke
Geoff Cottrell
Ronald Creighton
Jim Crossley
Barry Crowe
Margot Cutt (Sandal Wakefield)
J John Dale
Jeanette Carolyn Daly
Andrew and Liz Dawson
Colin Dawson
Keith and Joan Dinsdale
John Disney
John And Frances Doyle
John Gregory Eldon
Allen Emmott
Ruth Errington
J Stuart Everitt
Michael Farrar
Jane Forsythe
Freda Foster
Robert and Diane Foster
Stephen Richard Gibson
David and Gillian

Cyril Girdler
Brian and Dorothy Goad
Alfred Gouldstone
Joyce Greatwood
Susan A Greenwood
Steve Gresswell
Paul Griffiths
G T Hall
Tony Hall (Ulverston)
Martin Hannon
Harden Coach House
Peter and Cynthia Hardyman
Jean M Harland
Richard Harrison
Tony Harrowsmith
Chris S Hartley
Hazel Harvey
Michael Harvey
Dr R A Hill
R J Hobden
John Hone
John Houghton
Doris Howey
Tony Hudson
Anne Huntley
Alan Inder
Sandra Jacklin
Dennis Jarrat
Harry Jevons
Sally Jevons
Stephen J Kell
Luke & Sarah Kellett
Peter Kelly
David King
Ian & Lynne King
Michael Kirk
Allen Kirkbride
Dr Kirkland
Hilary and Roger Kite
Ian G Laing

Lois Laird
Richard Atkinson Lambert
Rex Lanham
Alan Laughton
Jane Lawson
Doreen E Leach
Leigh and Roma
Robert and Christine Leith
Joyce I Lewis
Joan Lockwood
Arthur Longbottom
Jennifer Luxford
George MacDonald Ross
Derek Marriott
John & Judith Marriott
Keith Marriott
John Mason
Margaret Ann Maw
Keith McBride
Helen McCredie
Sue Melville
Dennis Metcalfe
Joan Metcalfe
George Michalowski
Ian Millington
D R Moad
Thomas Andrew Morley
David John Mounsey
John Mounsey
Bert Newstead
Adam C Norton
Patricia Ollerenshaw
Sheila Osgerby
Desmond Palmer
Penelope Palmer
Frank Paterson
Kenneth Pattinson
david W G Pearce
Lindsay & Stan Pears
Christine Audrey Pearson
Aniza and Andrew Peel
Anne Peel
Rosa and Bernard Peel

Dr Anne Vivienne Norah Pepper
Ray Philpotts
John W Pickard
N W Pickard
Barry Pocock
Anthony Podmore
Ray Potter
D Preston
Linda B L and John B Price
Graham Priestley
David Prothero
Terry & Brenda Raggett
Jim Ranson
Andrea L T Rayner
B M Redman
Charles and Claire Richardson
Kate Rhodes
Clive Robinson
Mr D Robinson
Peter Robinson
Pat Robson
Pauline Rogerson
Arthur Peter Russell
Martin and Mary Salvage
Jill Sandles
Jean Saville
M J Sewell
John M Sheard
Stephen Sheard
The Lord Shuttleworth
Brian Smith (Grandad)
Les and Margaret Smith
Pat and Peter Spawforth
Bryan Marwood Speight
Simon Stembridge
Steve Strong
Robin Stubbs
Alan Sutcliffe
Robert William Swain
Christine Swales
Melvyn Taylor
Graham Thomas
James Thornton

Jane Thornton
Jonathan Thornton
Margaret Thornton
Michael Todd
Ralph Tomlinson
Ken Unwin
Mrs Lorna Vickers
Angela Walls
Anne Walton
S A Wappal
Hilda Ward
Sarah Warnes
Alan & Shirley Watkinson
Richard A Waxham
Michael Weighell
Trevor Weighell
Peter Wetherill
David W Whitaker
Ian Whitaker
Robert White
K G & A E Whittington
Ellen C Wilkinson
Val Williamson
John Heart and Elisabeth Wilson
Judith Wilson
Daphne Witham
Emma Wood
Hermione Wood
Joan Wood
David M Woodhall CBE
John D Woodhall LLB
Mr Linton Woodman
Jenny Woosey
Norman and Joyce Wordsworth
Mrs V H Youell
Michael Young
Your Gift from the Wayfarers —
walking vacations since 1984
Patricia Mary Yule